MAKERS *of the* MUSLIM WORLD

Imam Shafi'i

TITLES IN THE MAKERS OF THE MUSLIM WORLD SERIES

Series Editor: Patricia Crone, Institute for Advanced Study, Princeton

Abd al-Ghani al-Nabulusi, Samer Akkach
'Abd al-Malik, Chase F. Robinson
Abd al-Rahman III, Maribel Fierro
Abu Nuwas, Philip Kennedy
Ahmad al-Mansur, Mercedes García-Arenal
Ahmad ibn Hanbal, Christopher Melchert
Ahmad Riza Khan Barelwi, Usha Sanyal
Akbar, André Wink
Al-Ma'mun, Michael Cooperson
Al-Mutanabbi, Margaret Larkin
Amir Khusraw, Sunil Sharma
Ashraf 'Ali Thanawi, Muhammad Qasim Zaman
Chinggis Khan, Michal Biran
El Hajj Beshir Agha, Jane Hathaway
Fazlallah Astarabadi and the Hurufis, Shazad Bashir
Ghazali, Eric Ormsby
Hasan al-Banna, Gudrun Krämer
Husain Ahmad Madani, Barbara Metcalf
Ibn 'Arabi, William C. Chittick
Ibn Fudi, Ahmad Dallal
Ikhwan al-Safa, Godefroid de Callatay
Imam Shafi'i, Kecia Ali
Karim Khan Zand, John R. Perry
Mehmed Ali, Khaled Fahmy
Mu'awiya ibn abi Sufyan, R. Stephen Humphreys
Muhammad Abduh, Mark Sedgwick
Nasser, Joel Gordon
Nazira Zeineddine, miriam cooke
Sa'di, Homa Katouzian
Shaykh Mufid, Tamima Bayhom-Daou
Usama ibn Munqidh, Paul M. Cobb

For current information and details of other books in the series, please visit www.oneworld-publications.com

MAKERS
of the
MUSLIM
WORLD

Imam Shafi'i: Scholar and Saint

KECIA ALI

ONEWORLD
ACADEMIC

IMAM SHAF'I

A Oneworld Book
First published by Oneworld Publications, 2011
Reprinted, 2020

© Kecia Ali 2011

All rights reserved
Copyright under Berne Convention
A CIP record for this title is available
from the British Library

ISBN 978-1-85168-438-0
eISBN 978-1-78074-004-1

Typeset by Jayvee, Trivandrum, India
Cover and text designed by Design Deluxe
Printed and Bound in Great Britain
by Clays Ltd, Elcograf S.p.A.

Oneworld Publications
10 Bloomsbury Street
London, WC1B 3SR
England

Stay up to date with the latest books,
special offers, and exclusive content from
Oneworld with our newsletter

Sign up on our website
oneworld-publications.com

"Biographies are full of verifiable facts, but they are also full of things that aren't there: absences, gaps, missing evidence, knowledge or information that has been passed from person to person, losing credibility or shifting shape along the way. Biographies, like lives, are made up of contested objects — relics, testimonies, versions, correspondences, the unverifiable."

Hermione Lee, Virginia Woolf's Nose

"That biography ... is a species of fiction-making is a truth so old that only a willed cultural amnesia can make it new."

Marjorie Garber in Mary Rhiel and David Suchoff, eds,
The Seductions of Biography

CONTENTS

Acknowledgements ix
Introduction xi

1 ARABIAN YEARS 1

2 FROM STUDENT TO SHAYKH 27

3 LEGAL THEORY I: THE *RISALA*, SUNNA, AND HADITH 47

4 LEGAL THEORY II: ANALOGY, *IJTIHAD*, AND CONSENSUS 69

5 THE *UMM* AND SUBSTANTIVE LAW 79

6 SAINT SHAFI'I 99

   CONCLUSION 113

Further Reading 117
Bibliography 121
Index 131

ACKNOWLEDGEMENTS

Vincent Cornell introduced me to Shafiʿi and his *Risala* in a graduate seminar in 1997; it was not love at first page. But when I was invited to contribute a biography to this series, I recklessly proposed Shafiʿi, whose writings on positive law had entranced me in my research on marriage and about whose life I knew almost nothing. Since then, Emad Adly, Jonathan Brockopp, Ahmed El Shamsy, Kevin Jaques, Joseph Lowry, Christopher Melchert, Kevin Reinhart, and David Vishanoff have discussed Shafiʿi's ideas and writings and tangled life story with me, suggested important sources, and shared forthcoming publications. The bibliography imperfectly indicates my numerous debts to them. Patricia Crone, Anver Emon, and Oneworld's anonymous reader provided thorough and thoughtful comments on the entire manuscript, and saved me from mistakes and misjudgments. Oneworld's Paul Boone shepherded the project through numerous delays and Sophie Richmond provided meticulous copyediting. None of these people bears any blame for remaining errors, of which I hope there are few, or inadequacies, of which I am sure there are many. I also owe thanks to my research assistant Matthew Pierce, who hunted down obscure Orientalist publications and put order to towering piles of photocopies; Emine Fetvaci, who provided a wonderful illustration; and Mara Worle and Amr Ragy, who hosted me during a visit to Cairo where I visited Shafiʿi's tomb. In addition to drawing my attention to a useful article, Malik Khan of the Islamic Center of Boston – Wayland invited me to speak to the congregation during Ramadan 2007 about Shafiʿi's thought. It is to the members of that community, engaged in a collective struggle to live according to God's plan – and disagreeing, sometimes profoundly, over what that entails – that this book is dedicated.

INTRODUCTION

How should Muslims live? In accordance with God's law. How can one know God's law? First and foremost through the Qur'an. But the Qur'an, though expansive, is not exhaustive. People need supplementary guidance. The most widely accepted source for additional guidance is the Prophet Muhammad's model or *sunna*. Beyond his role as a conduit for God's speech, Muhammad's conduct as a man and as leader of an exemplary community carries weight. Within a couple of centuries of his death, reports about his words and deeds, known as *hadith*, came to play a vital role in preaching, moral instruction, scriptural commentary, and – most significant for purposes of this story – lawmaking. The central role of prophetic sunna in legal theory is in large part due to the work of Muhammad ibn Idris al-Shafi'i. Shafi'i lived from 150/767 to 204/820, when Islamic law was in its formative stages. He was preoccupied with the question of how to derive rules for conduct from God's communication to humanity. The now-besieged notion of the partnership of Qur'an and sunna, which structured Sunni thinking for more than a millennium, largely derives from his intellectual labor. One must understand his ideas and their impact to understand Islamic law.

Until recently, conventional wisdom has held that Shafi'i's *Risala* or *Epistle*, a treatise on legal theory, offered a solution to the dichotomous thinking that plagued his contemporaries. According to this view they were hopelessly divided between traditionalists and partisans of opinion. The former, often identified with Medina, were intent on strictly applying precedent of the Prophet or his Companions, those Muslims who had known him personally. The latter, associated with Iraq, were advocates of reasoned opinion or *ra'y*, and allowed individual discretion in judgment – a surefire path to interpretive chaos, in the view of some. Neither position was tenable, given competing needs to establish predictable rules that respected religious sources while also responding to changing conditions of life in the rapidly expanding Abbasid Empire. Shafi'i – "the *deus ex machina* of his time" in Noel Coulson's memorable if hyperbolic phrase – resolved the dilemma by pairing a strict reliance on revealed texts with a restricted form of analogical reasoning (Coulson 1964, 53). The heroic synthesis he supposedly wrought between the advocates of "opinion" (*ahl al-ra'y*) and the partisans of hadith (*ahl al-hadith*) led to accolades such as "without doubt the single greatest Islamic legal scholar" and "Allah's gift to Islamic jurisprudence."

This book tells a somewhat different story. It is true Shafi'i was in some sense a compromiser and that his legal theory had a major impact on the development of Islamic thought. His crucial contribution, however, was not the four-source theory of the law (Qur'an, prophetic sunna, *qiyas* – strict reasoning based on revealed texts, consensus) with which textbooks credit him; in fact, his architecture of the law looked somewhat different. Moreover, the story which opposes traditionalist Medina to rationalist Iraq both ignores the fact that the Medinans used reason and the Iraqis appealed to precedent, and obscures a wider web of thriving, contentious bodies of scholars in Mecca, Medina, Iraq, and Egypt who had competing ideas about authority, precedent, and the role of human reason.

Rather than brokering a definitive compromise between two warring factions, Shafi'i drew from a variety of teachers and his exposure to various currents of thought to formulate his theory of the law, which rejected what he saw as equally unsatisfactory tendencies to rely on communal sensibilities or individual reasoning unmoored from revelation. Instead, he borrowed technical terms from grammarians and rhetorical strategies from theologians. He involved himself in sometimes rancorous disputes with other jurists. His interlocutors pushed him to define his ideas and helped shape the broader parameters of legal scholarship of the time. My central aim in this book is to explicate and analyse his legal activity and its written traces. What debates did he intervene in? What kinds of arguments did he use and how successful were they? What solutions did he propose to the methodological quandaries of his colleagues? Did he apply them himself in his own decision-making? And how did his legal ideas mesh with broader conceptions about the nature of God and humanity, as well as the proper relations between them?

Shafi'i considered law vital to social and cosmic order. He placed law at the heart of Muslim life since the key obligation of each Muslim was to obey God. God's plan culminated in the law, perhaps the most satisfying and important of not only human but also divine endeavors: it is through the law that human beings fulfill their duty of obedience. Shafi'i's views about law are central to this book, but I also give an overview of his life and, in a way, his afterlife. He became the posthumous "patron saint" of a legal school; twelve centuries after his death he remains a figure of popular interest and veneration. Egyptians visit his tomb in droves and write to him seeking his intercession in their affairs. In Indonesia, where the legal school named for him claims dominance over the world's largest Muslim population, pious biographies in Bahasa grace booksellers' stalls. The Internet makes conversation about him global. Bilingual English and Arabic websites invite readers to submit their favorite poems by him and lay Muslims press his opinions into service for vigorous online debates about Sufism and shrine visitation as well as a host of other topics.

Who was this man who garners such devotion and so many attempts to coopt his authority? Any narrative of Shafi'i's life must be tentative in many of its particulars, though not because biographical treatments of his life are scarce; to the contrary, they are plentiful. They care little for intimate matters, so our knowledge of his domestic arrangements is sketchy, limited to a handful of terse facts about his four children and their two mothers. We know substantially more about his career: names of teachers and students, places he lectured, books he authored. But the sources on his professional life are formulaic and hagiographic, making them difficult to weigh.

Our information on him comes from two types of sources. First is the characteristic Muslim genre, the biographical dictionary. These works arrange notices alphabetically or by generation, for subjects selected by profession, genealogy, place of residence, or other defining characteristic. They relay information through recognized authorities, attesting to their information's trustworthiness through authenticated processes of transmission. The material itself is far from transparent, though. Compilers exercised a great deal of license in composing entries, choosing what to put in and leave out and how to frame stories. In trying to augment one person's prestige, they might downplay the achievements of or snipe at a rival. The second type of source is even more skewed: the *Virtues* (*Manaqib*) writings dedicated to prominent figures. Although the content of these works shifts over time, they often reproduce stock tropes rather than recount individual experience, producing something more like Dr. Johnson's "universal panegyrick" than psychologically acute portraits of their individual subjects. They are not devoid of facts – they are full of them! – but factual accuracy is not their primary aim.

Because of the difficult nature of the sources, a ritual disclaimer precedes modern Western attempts to reconstruct Shafi'i's life story: "A great mass of legend has grown up around his life," W. Heffening offers as an opening sally in the *Encyclopaedia of Islam*, "and it is difficult to sift out the really historical matter." Even setting pious aggrandizing aside, the traditional sources are treacherous. Anticipating the postmodern turn by centuries, authors refused to smooth over variations and contradictions to provide linear narrative and coherent characterization. More troublesome, competing versions of the basic facts exist even as to the "really historical matter."

His biographers agree on a few things. He was an Arab of the Prophet's tribe. He spent his childhood in the Arabian peninsula. He was educated in Mecca and Medina, studied and taught in Iraq, and eventually moved to Cairo. There he taught, refined his doctrines, died, and was buried. Nearly everything else about his life is debated, especially the chronology of his travels. His birthplace is uncertain and his mother's ancestry disputed. A sojourn in the Yemen, if not entirely fictitious, might have been devoted to study, employment, or fomenting rebellion. Whether he had one or two periods of residence in Egypt is unclear. His death was due either to illness or to mob violence. To lay out all variants let alone carefully weigh each possibility would require a massive study. Since controversies over biographical minutiae alternately absorb and stymie a small cadre of specialists but are of little interest for general readers, I have sometimes simply presented what seems to me the most likely story. At other times, I have laid out possible paths with some of the supporting evidence. As to that evidence, one cannot responsibly dodge the issue of source reliability entirely, but I have said far less about it than I might have. We still await a study of the shifting treatment of Shafi'i in Muslim biographical sources. The general trend of studies in the field has been toward discerning the complex structure and implicit messages of biographical texts (and chronicles) rather than using them as repositories of historical fact. Still, although the sources for Shafi'i's life are highly partisan, deeply contradictory, and often tendentious, they are not pure literary construction: there is a man there, somewhere, and I hope to have enabled glimpses of him.

NOTE ON TRANSLATION, TRANSLITERATION, SOURCES, AND DATES

Most of the primary sources for Shafi'i's life and work are available only in Arabic. Where possible, I have quoted from translations, sometimes with modifications, and given references to English sources to make things easier for non-specialists. Unless noted, other translations from Arabic scriptural, legal, and biographical texts, and from secondary works in European languages, are my own. Suggestions for further reading appear after the text. Full information for works cited parenthetically and the scholarly publications on which I have relied most heavily can be found in the bibliography, along with a list of abbreviations used in the text. As the format of this series does not allow for notes, I invite those who would like specific references to contact me in care of the publisher.

I have kept Arabic terminology to a minimum but give Arabic terms along with their English counterparts where the latter are ambiguous. A few terms, like *hadith* and *sunna*, make frequent appearances and I have not italicized them after their first use. I omit diacritics except ' for 'ayn and ' for hamza. (The bibliography retains full transliteration.) I have also taken the liberty of standardizing transliterations and dropping the definite article (al- or ash-) in quotations, thus al-Shāfi'ī and Šāfi'ī (and ash-Shafe'ee, etc.) all become Shafi'i.

Muslims use a lunar calendar that dates from Muhammad's emigration (*hijra*) to Medina in 622 CE. I usually give both *hijri* and common era dates, thus: 204/820, the year of Shafi'i's death. When the specific month and day of an occurrence is unknown, conversion can be imprecise so common era years appear as ranges. References to centuries are likewise inexact, but the second century *hijri* when he was born corresponds roughly to the eighth century CE.

ARABIAN YEARS

Everyone agrees where Shafi'i died but no one is quite certain where he was born. A short narration of his life, extracted from a sea of hagiographical material in the massive biographical compendium of Ibn Khallikan (d. 681/1283), begins by alluding to these controversies:

> His birth was in the year 150, and it has been said that he was born on the day Abu Hanifa died. His birth was in the city of Gaza. Some have said in Ashkelon, and some have said in Yemen, but the first is sounder. He was taken from Gaza to Mecca when he was a boy of two and raised there. He recited the Noble Qur'an. The account of his journey to study with Malik ibn Anas is famous and there is no need to tell it at length. He arrived in Baghdad in the year 195 and stayed there two years, then left for Mecca. He returned to Baghdad in 198 and stayed there a month, then left for Egypt. He arrived there in 199, though some say 201. He stayed there until he died on Friday, the last day of Rajab in the year 204. He was buried after the afternoon prayer that day in the Lesser Qarafa. His grave, near Mount Muqattam, is visited [by the pious]. May God be pleased with him.
>
> (IK 23)

This sketch does not mention a sojourn in Yemen or a spell with the Bedouin, and some would quibble over dates, but this is a reasonable summary of his trajectory: from Palestine to Mecca to Medina to Iraq, back to Mecca, back to Iraq, and finally to Egypt. Ibn Abi Hatim al-Razi's (d. 326–7/938) catalogue of *Shafi'i's Manners and Virtues*, our earliest relatively full biographical source, mentions the two possibilities which Ibn Khallikan rejects. "I was born in Yemen," Shafi'i here declares. Or, alternately, "I was born in Ashkelon" (IAH 21). (Ashkelon is a town not far from Gaza.) Gaza becomes standard by the time medieval biographers compose their accounts. The mention of Yemen is explained as a reference to his mother's presumed Yemeni ancestry. Occasionally, some have cited the town of Mina near Mecca as his birthplace, but I will assume that he is Palestinian-born.

SHAFI'I'S ANCESTRY

Of his father, we know only his impeccable Arab pedigree and that he died when Shafi'i was young. Shafi'i explained his impoverished mother's decision to move to Mecca once she was left with charge of her young son – most agree with Ibn Khallikan that the move took place when he was two, although a few accounts say ten – as a means of claiming his birthright. Shafi'i's full name, and hence genealogy, is: Muhammad ibn Idris ibn al-'Abbas ibn 'Uthman ibn Shafi' ibn al-Sa'ib ibn 'Ubayd ibn 'Abd Yazid ibn Hashim ibn al-Mutallib ibn 'Abd Manaf al-Qurashi al-Mutallibi, Abu 'Abdallah al-Shafi'i al-Makki. That is to say, he is Muhammad, the son of Idris, the son of al-'Abbas etc., of the Mutallib clan of the Quraysh tribe. His appellation "Abu 'Abdallah," sometimes used by colleagues, was given by the time he was in his teens, before any of his children were born; it expressed hope that he would father a son who would, as the name 'Abdallah implies, be a devoted servant of God. His wife apparently called him Ibn Idris, as did others on occasion. His colleagues and students usually referred to him as Shafi'i, as I will. It means "intercessor."

Shafi'i's lineage was particularly illustrious. Though he was not a direct descendant of the Prophet, they shared a tribe (Quraysh) as well as an ancestor ('Abd Manaf). The Prophet's great-grandfather Hashim was the brother of al-Mutallib, Shafi'i's many-times great grandfather. 'Abd Manaf had two other sons but the connection between the Prophet's clan and Shafi'i's clan was close. Muhammad reportedly once declared that "The Hashim clan and the Mutallib clan are one and the same" (Abu Zahra 1948, 15; IAH 123). Shafi'i's sobriquet "the Mutallibi" emphasizes this noble origin. His connection to the Prophet is also played up in the designation "the Prophet's cousin" (*ibn 'am Rasulallah*), literally "son of the paternal uncle of the Messenger of God." Both names continue to be used to the present day. (Occasional later detractors asserted that his tie to the tribe was one of clientage not descent. In seeking to disparage him, presumably groundlessly, these charges point to the cachet Arab heritage conferred.)

Between 'Abd Manaf in the remote past and Shafi'i's immediate progenitors there were a few notable figures. His great-great-great-grandfather Sa'ib ibn 'Ubayd served as Hashemite standard-bearer at the decisive battle of Badr (2/624), where the Muslims trounced their Meccan opponents. Taken prisoner, Sa'ib ransomed himself and then converted to Islam. Since Muslims customarily freed converts without payment, Sa'ib was asked why he did not convert immediately. He replied that he did not want to deprive the Muslims of benefits expected from the ransom. The other ancestral accomplishment routinely mentioned along with Shafi'i's genealogy is that, as a young man, Sa'ib's son Shafi', Shafi'i's great-great-grandfather, once met the Prophet.

Befitting someone with his background, Shafi'i became an expert in genealogy. Knowing names and ancestors helped keep track of those who reported on the deeds of the Prophet. It also mattered for assessing people. Shafi'i was unencumbered by any notion of the innate equality of all humankind, except perhaps in a general religious sense. Like many of his contemporaries, he thought that Arabs were inherently superior to non-Arabs in certain respects — linguistic competence being perhaps the most important — and that some Arabs were superior to others. His genealogical expertise was not limited to patrilineal descent. After an all-nighter spent discussing women's lineages with colleagues, he scoffed, "Anyone can know men's lineages" (B 1:489).

In Shafi'i's case, it is his mother's ancestry rather than his father's that provokes speculation. She probably belonged to the Yemeni 'Azd tribe. A colorful but unlikely account traces her descent in a direct male line from 'Ali ibn Abi Talib's union with the Prophet's daughter Fatima, making her the Prophet's great-great-granddaughter and linking her to the "people of the house," a phrase reserved for the Prophet's family, specifically 'Ali – who was the Prophet's paternal cousin as well as his son-in-law – Fatima, and their children. Fatima would thus have been not only Shafi'i's mother's ancestor but also her namesake. An alternate genealogy provides an additional link to 'Ali through one of Shafi'i's aunts, making his connection to 'Ali even closer than his connection to the Prophet. Shafi'i may be "the Prophet's paternal cousin" but 'Ali, in this telling, is his cousin twice over. Regardless of whether he has a double helping of Hashemite ancestry, the closeness between Shafi'i and 'Ali is played up repeatedly, including in a series of dreams he reportedly experienced.

EARLY EDUCATION

Shafi'i's lineage is of great interest to his traditional biographers; his childhood is not. Modern biography roots adult life choices in the psychologically formative experiences of youth, granting early influences premium explanatory power. In contrast, premodern Arabic biography reports little beyond the conventional about anyone's childhood. We possess only a few formulaic anecdotes about his early years, involving his primary religious education and his aristocratic pursuits including archery and poetry.

He grew up poor in Mecca's Shi'b al-Khayf neighborhood. He obtained an education at the local Qur'an school (*kuttab*) despite his straitened circumstances. Since his mother could not afford to pay the instructor, Shafi'i earned his keep by tutoring the younger students. He memorized the Qur'an by age seven, an age that recurs in scholarly biographies. He then recited it before Isma'il ibn

'Abdullah ibn Qustantin, a leading Meccan authority on *qira'at* (readings or recitations of the Qur'an) who was also a grammarian. Shafi'i was thus initiated into the practice of authorized oral transmission that characterized religious scholarship.

In the second half of the eighth century, when Shafi'i began his study of the religious sciences, Mecca was an important center for scholarship. Medina, where he later studied, had been the Muslims' capital during the lifetime of the Prophet and his immediate successors. The Umayyads (661–750) had moved the capital to Damascus. Around 762, a dozen years after the Abbasid revolution and five years before Shafi'i's birth, the caliph al-Mansur (r. 136–58/ 754–75) shifted the imperial capital to the newly founded Baghdad, where Shafi'i – or so the story goes – would eventually appear before his grandson Harun al-Rashid (r. 170–93/786–809). But Mecca remained important despite its distance from the court. Some Meccan scholars descended from the Prophet's Companions; others had migrated to the city. Pilgrims from throughout the increasingly vast Muslim empire became part of the immense transfer and exchange of knowledge from one generation to the next and from one part of the world to another.

Scholarly activity flourished in Mecca's main mosque near the Ka'ba. In addition to serving as places of communal prayer, mosques were bases for trading and socializing, as well as the primary location where secondary religious instruction took place. Designated locations within the mosque housed teaching circles. Precise etiquettes attended such gatherings. These included the placement of groupings within the mosque space – some pillars were more prestigious than others; some circles needed more space than others – and the position of listeners relative to the teacher.

At the mosque, Shafi'i began his advanced lessons which included the study of hadith (reports about the Prophet and his Companions) and investigation of their precedents and responses on matters of legal import. Shafi'i's teachers included two Meccan scholars of particular repute. Muslim ibn Khalid al-Zanji (d. 179/795 or 180/796) was mufti (jurisconsult) of the city. He first authorized Shafi'i to deliver legal opinions (*fatwas*) at the tender age of fifteen or eighteen: "Give fatwas, Abu 'Abdallah" (Ibn Hajar 1994, 24). Sufyan ibn 'Uyayna (d. 198/814) was a renowned Kufan-born hadith scholar whom Shafi'i reportedly declared better at explaining hadith and more qualified to give legal opinions than anyone else he had ever met. He is also known for having had an interest in exegetical (*tafsir*) traditions, and it may have been through him that Shafi'i developed his abiding interest in matters concerned with Qur'an interpretation and the narratives associated with the revelation of specific passages.

Despite his intellectual aptitude, Shafi'i continued to face economic obstacles to pursuing his education. His mother did not have enough money to purchase papyrus so he was forced to take notes haphazardly, scribbling on pieces of bone or writing on his own forearm in saliva. Accounts which tell of the latter are, perhaps, less interested in his improvised writing implements than in making the point that his memory was so prodigious that he could memorize things written in that fashion before the spit had dried.

DESERT WANDERINGS

It was desirable for urban Arabs of noble descent to perfect their Arabic in the desert, free from the corrupting influences of foreign dialects that had infiltrated the language of cities and towns. A period of fostering with a Bedouin tribe was a rite of passage for elite boys. At some point before or after his Meccan studies, Shafi'i reportedly lived with the Hudhayl tribe, whom he describes as "the most eloquent of the Arabs." There, he learned martial skills such as horsemanship, without distinguishing himself particularly, and archery. He was a passionate and skilled archer. He reports practicing "until I was hitting the bull's eye ten times out of ten" (Ibn Hajar 1994, 24). A more modest report has nine times out of ten – more plausible, still impressive. Shafi'i's reputation as an archer survived the centuries. The fourteenth-century Ottoman author Yunani includes in his treatise on military and recreational archery an anecdote where Shafi'i encounters a descendant of Sa'd ibn Abi Waqqas, who wielded bow and arrow in defense of the Prophet at the Battle of 'Uhud (3/625), and proves his own merit to her by listing essential practices for an archer.

Poetry was Shafi'i's other pursuit during these years. An account on the authority of his grandson Muhammad, identified as "the son of Shafi'i's daughter" rather than by patronymic, says that Shafi'i spent two decades learning Arabic and tribal stories with the Hudhayl. Another source says seventeen years. He mastered the Hudhayl poetic canon, memorizing, it is said, 10,000 lines of their tribal poetry. It is more plausible – if in fact the interlude is not pure invention – that he studied Qur'an and hadith in Mecca and then spent several years in the desert learning poetry and "Bedouin stories" (*ayyam al-'arab*) before returning to Mecca to resume or begin his study of jurisprudence.

As an adult, Shafi'i continued to compose and recite poetry. His biographers laud his skill in poetic memorization, recitation, and composition. Ibn Khallikan reports that even the luminary al-Asma'i (d. 213/828) read Hudhayl poems under Shafi'i's supervision. Rather than seeing in poetry a detour from the path of religious knowledge, his contemporaries saw it as a complementary pursuit. Indeed, it is difficult to overstate the importance of linguistic mastery to the Arab intellectual elite of the time. Poetry was inextricably linked to the Arabic language, and language to revelation. Shafi'i sprinkles his legal writings with couplets of his own composition, to elucidate points of usage or to add literary savor. His poetic dabbling was not unique; many respectable scholars wrote poetry which their biographers quote, sometimes at length. Shafi'i was not known for the lewd verse that even some scholars with impeccable reputations composed, much less the kind that characterized the oeuvre of his contemporary, the bawdy poet Abu Nuwas. Instead, the *Diwan* or *Collected Poems* attributed to Shafi'i ranges over many themes but lingers over knowledge and its opposite. Shafi'i elsewhere reportedly deemed seeking knowledge preferable to voluntary prayer.

JOURNEY TO MEDINA

Shafi'i soon departed for Medina, the first destination on his "journey in search of knowledge" (*rihla li talab al-'ilm*). Medina's reputation as a center for religious learning was consolidated during the lifetime of Malik ibn Anas (d. 179/796). Born between 90 and 97 hijri (708–16 CE), Malik studied with several respected Successors (the generation after the Companions) and those of the following generation. Malik became the most reliable source for Medinan positions on legal matters of ritual, commerce, and family. His book the *Muwatta'* (*The Well-Trodden Path* or *The Approved*) conveys the legal state of affairs in Medina. Organized by topic, it includes statements transmitted directly from Muhammad, the views of his Companions – including their occasional disagreements – and the doctrines of earlier Medinan authorities. Its major goal is to establish the authoritative practice of the local community, felt best to represent the Prophet's example. Often, discussion of a point will be summed up with Malik's statement affirming a local consensus: "That is the way we do things."

Shafi'i was apparently already acquainted with the *Muwatta'* when he set out to meet Malik. In one version, Shafi'i seeks letters of introduction from the governor of Mecca to the governor of Medina and Malik himself. In another, Shafi'i is an importunate youngster whose only recommendation is his familiarity with Malik's work, obtained from a text he borrowed. Shafi'i recalls: "I came to Malik ibn Anas, and I had memorized the *Muwatta'*. He said to me, I will find someone to recite it to you. I said, I can recite it. So I recited the *Muwatta'* to him from memory (*hafizan*)" (IK 22). In other versions of this anecdote, Malik takes more persuading before he eventually relents and permits Shafi'i to recite the text. He does so flawlessly. Malik is reluctantly but thoroughly impressed. At one point, Shafi'i intends to stop reciting but, he recalls, "the beauty of my recitation pleased him and he said, 'Continue, young man'" ('Abd al-Salam 1988, 43).

ORAL AND WRITTEN

This encounter highlights the complicated interplay between written texts and oral performances of these texts. When he seeks out Malik, the senior scholar assumes that Shafi'i should follow the usual procedure of having one of Malik's disciples recite the text to him. This mode of transmission, where the scholar recites and the student listens is known as *sama'* or "hearing." (If a text was involved, students would check their copy of the text against the teacher's lecture.) Shafi'i was able, instead, to proceed by *qira'a*, reading of the text back to the scholar. Though he recollects reciting the *Muwatta'* by heart, more usually students would read a text they had copied back to the teacher, so that the teacher could correct mistakes. (Texts could also be transmitted by dictation [*imla'*], and students could also simply take lecture notes while listening to a scholar speak, possibly from prepared notes.)

Gregor Schoeler has written extensively on the question of oral and written transmission in early Islamic history. In his view, lectures delivered from written notes were more frequent than those delivered from memory. Notebooks certainly served as reminders, especially given the length and complexity of texts under study. These notebooks could be used to refresh one's own memory or teach later students, as well as eventually to circulate works in a more polished form. The production of written texts from oral encounters was a key element of early legal practice. Shafi'i undoubtedly relied on notes in giving some of his lectures and, as we will see later, Shafi'i's main work of substantive law is based on the detailed lecture notes of one of his students. Authorship was sometimes a collective endeavor, with author and transmitter not entirely distinguished until decades or perhaps a century after his lifetime.

Some texts were simply transmitted from writing to writing without the safeguard of oral checking and, possibly, elaboration. One might make a copy for oneself or pay a professional copyist. But in both hadith scholarship and in the emerging discipline of jurisprudence, direct contact between teacher and student was vital. William Graham's notion of an "*isnad* paradigm" can be helpful in understanding why this was so. The term *isnad*, which means support, comes from hadith scholarship. A hadith comprises two parts: the textual content (*matn*), which conveys information, and the *isnad*, which supports the text. It refers to the list of transmitters who pass along a report from someone who heard the Prophet say, or saw him do, something noteworthy. The notion of a chain of transmitters, whose sincerity, reliability, and uprightness guarantees the validity of what they transmit has purchase, Graham argues, far beyond the narrow purview of hadith study. He suggests the much wider acceptance among Muslims of a "fundamental presupposition that truth does not reside in documents, however authentic, ancient, or well-preserved, but in authentic human beings and their personal connections with one another." One requires not documents alone but "a line of *persons* possessed of *both* knowledge and righteousness to teach and convey them across the years" for "authoritative transmission." The personal link between student and teacher "guarantees the faithful copying, memorizing, reciting, and understanding of texts – not only those of the Hadith, but those of the Qur'an and all subsequent works of Muslim piety and learning" (Graham 1993, 507).

MALIK AND HADITH

Unlike disciplines such as grammar, philosophy, and medicine, jurisprudence is one of the religious sciences to which the *isnad* paradigm applies. Hadith and jurisprudence were intimately related in Malik's scholarship: he did not divide hadith with formal chains of authorities linking them back to the Prophet or his Companions from other types of authority statements in his *Muwatta'* (nor did he or anyone else at the time make a major distinction between hadith going back to the Prophet and those going back to his Companions). Despite the high regard in which later hadith scholars held him, Malik himself did not identify sunna narrowly with hadith reports, nor did he limit sunna to the practice of the Prophet alone. Rather, Malik and other Medinan authorities upheld the town's practice (*'amal*) – or at least what they saw as the authoritative practice of the town – even when this seemed to contradict accounts of the Prophet's spoken words or actual deeds. They considered prophetic precedent to be more reliably preserved in the living tradition of the Medinan community than in words transmitted from one individual to another.

Hadith scholarship developed considerably in the decades after Shafi'i, in part in response to his influential redefinition of hadith reports as the sole authoritative repository of prophetic example, which he considered crucial to jurisprudence. The two giants of Sunni hadith scholarship, Muhammad al-Bukhari (d. 256/870) and Muslim ibn Hajjaj (d. 261/875), would put together their compilations of sound hadith. Known as the "two sound ones" (*sahihayn*), *Sahih Bukhari* and *Sahih Muslim* attained a canonical status alongside several other compendia. These were not the first compilations of hadith, but they represented a new stage of canonization and of a developing division of labor between hadith scholars and jurists.

But during Malik's lifetime, the circulation of hadith reports in written form was innovative. Writing hadith had been, briefly, controversial. These debates over writing were sometimes charged with theological significance. A fairly short-lived current worried that a written canon of prophetic hadith might rival the Qur'an. There were also specific practical concerns about written transmission. Could information be fruitfully and faithfully transmitted by writing alone? What type of interaction between narrators was required to constitute a strong link? These issues of hadith reliability became central to Shafi'i's legal methodology as he singled out prophetic hadith as vital to law. Nonetheless, Shafi'i's genius did not lie in the collection and transmission of hadith. Although he learned traditions through his life, including from Malik, and related them as textual support for legal arguments, he was more concerned with the role and function of hadith in legal reasoning. Shafi'i incorporated the hadith he learned into his own jurisprudence, but never became a transmitter or critic of note. Neither Bukhari nor Muslim includes reports on his authority in their compilations. Malik, by contrast, figures prominently.

Malik was more than a hadith scholar. He influenced other jurists including Muhammad al-Shaybani (d. 189/805), who would eventually become Shafi'i's sparring partner and teacher, and Ibn 'Abd al-Hakam (d. 214/829), with whom Shafi'i later stayed in Egypt. Though, like Shafi'i, Ibn 'Abd al-Hakam did not transmit the *Muwatta'*, he became a Maliki scholar of some repute whose *Digest* preserves a substantial amount of Malik's teaching.

Conflicting accounts make it impossible to say precisely when Shafi'i arrived in Medina or exactly when he left or where he went next. One scholar suggests that Shafi'i went to Medina at the age of twenty-three and studied with Malik for only four years before leaving for Yemen. Other accounts send him to Medina as early as age thirteen and keep him there much longer. In this view, Shafi'i would have passed directly from study of the Qur'an to study of the *Muwatta'*, which one report says he memorized at the age of ten. But neither of these chronologies quite accounts for other data. He spent a good bit of time in Mecca with his teachers and possibly several years in the desert with the Bedouin – though the desert sojourn is a topos, it is plausible. Thus, we should reject the view that he spent nearly two decades in Medina. On the other hand, a few years would not suffice for the deep engagement Shafi'i's substantive and theoretical writings show with Malik and his ideas. It seems likeliest to me that Shafi'i came to Medina at around age twenty, around 170/787, and spent about a decade with Malik. Malik – assuming one trusts the traditional reports of his longevity – would have been in his late sixties or early seventies when Shafi'i arrived. No doubt Malik's elder-statesman status helps to account for Shafi'i's continued deference toward him in his later career, even as he criticized some of his doctrines and methods. Though he reportedly praised the *Muwatta'* lavishly ("I don't know any book of knowledge on earth which brings more reward than Malik's book"), he would eventually criticize Malik's emphasis on community precedent alongside Iraqi proponents of a related view: that the accepted view of a particular group of scholars was authoritative. Still, Shafi'i's journey to Medina to study with Malik was one of the defining moments of his life; it set the stage for his subsequent intellectual development.

YEMEN AND IRAQ

Shafi'i probably remained in Medina until Malik's death in 179/795. Then, nearing thirty, he moved on. He may have returned, briefly, to Mecca before setting out again to Yemen, for study or government service or both, then traveling on to Iraq. A poem attributed to Shafi'i enumerates the positive effects of travel:

> Leave your homeland and go abroad in search of advancement!
> Go and travel, for travel has five benefits:
> Relief from worries, gain of a livelihood,
> knowledge, education, and keeping company with good men.
> (Rosenthal 1957, 51)

It is unclear which of these benefits he sought from his journey to Yemen. Two explanations predominate. One view is that he went to Yemen as part of his pursuit of knowledge. The other explanation is that he joined the retinue of a newly appointed governor to Yemen, when the appointee passed through the Hijaz – that is, the western part of the Arabian peninsula, home to Mecca and Medina – on his way to take up his post.

Attempting to sort fact from legend in the accounts of Shafi'i's Yemeni travels, Wadad al-Qadi has suggested that perhaps he made two trips. In an early journey, he mastered the Yemeni dialect and pursued his far-flung interests in areas including physiognomy, medicine, and astronomy. Physiognomy (*firasa*) was the science of using people's physical characteristics to assess character and temperament. Shafi'i claims to have traveled to Yemen to procure books on the subject. Physiognomy had existed at the margins of jurisprudence for some time; the Prophet's Companions relied on it from time to time to sort out paternity claims. Shafi'i is sometimes said to have disavowed physiognomy, though a sixteenth-century Egyptian treatise considers him an authority: "Our Imam Shafi'i has said: a long nose with a thin tip is an indication of fickleness and stupidity and irascibility."

Shafi'i was also interested in prophetic medicine, pharmacology, and "the science of the stars," though some say his early interest in star-science morphed into disapproval. Unlike physiognomy and star-science, medicine entails no controversy. Shafi'i praises medicine, stating "Knowledge is of two types: religious knowledge and worldly knowledge. Religious knowledge is jurisprudence and worldly knowledge is medicine" (IAH 321). This is quite an encomium from a man who thinks law the supreme science. His specific medical advice includes tidbits on the merits of eating beans. He also collected strange facts and odd tales, to which he makes offhand references in the *Umm* and in the recollections of his colleagues and students. One of his Egyptian students reports Shafi'i's astonishing discovery that Yemeni females could become pregnant at age nine; he also met a twenty-one-year-old grandmother. He sought other empirical data, too, such as how much the Prophet collected in poll tax from the various provinces. If one posits a longer stay in Yemen, it is also possible that his language and poetry study was with Yemenis rather than with the Hudhayl tribe. (If so, his time with them would be part of a later reconstruction of his biography to conform to the prophetic model, including a period of Bedouin fostering.)

In addition to his pursuits of general knowledge, he also reportedly sought religious learning at the feet of noted scholars. Fakhr al-Din al-Razi (d. 606/1209) includes among Shafi'i's nineteen most significant teachers four Yemenis alongside five Meccans, six Medinans, and four Iraqis. It is sometimes said that Mutarrif ibn Mazin, the judge of Sana'a, was one of Shafi'i's Yemeni teachers. None of these teachers, however, seems to have had the kind of influence on his thought that his Meccan, Medinan, and Iraqi teachers did. Given Shafi'i's inclinations toward amassing knowledge and refining his learning, it would be uncharacteristic for him to travel somewhere new and not obtain as much new material as possible in any field he thought worthy, even if formal study was not his primary objective. Another of his poems states:

> Whoever does not taste the momentary bitterness of learning
> Will all his life swallow the humiliation of ignorance.
>
> *(Diwan* 29)

Whether his studies were ancillary to his employment or whether they were carried out in separate trips, his fraught relationship with the government led to a major upheaval in his life. Biographer Claire Harman states that "some things become less knowable about a subject the more data accrues around them" (2005, xvii). Shafi'i's Yemeni adventures (and maybe misadventures) attest to the truth of her statement.

'ALID LOYALTIES AND REBELLION

In order to understand the muddled allegations surrounding Shafi'i's encounter with intrigue, it is necessary to sketch the prevailing political and social context more fully. The Abbasid caliph al-Mansur's reign of two decades had ended in 158/775 when his son al-Mahdi (r. 158/775–169/785) succeeded him. In 170/786, after a brief skirmish over succession, al-Mahdi's son Harun al-Rashid ascended to the throne at the age of twenty. Harun's twenty-three-year reign is the setting for many tales in *The 1001 Arabian Nights*. He governed from a metropolis that was the center of the civilized world. Though firm demographic data are impossible to obtain, during this period Baghdad probably eclipsed Xi'an in China as the world's largest city – a spot it maintained for two centuries – with a population estimated at between 700,000 and one million. It was rivaled in the premodern Muslim world only by Cordoba, at the height of Andalusia's Golden Age in the tenth and eleventh centuries, and Istanbul, during the sixteenth-century apex of the Ottoman Empire.

Early Abbasid caliphs sought political and administrative centralization while patronizing cultural and scholarly endeavors. An increasingly authoritarian administration aimed to consolidate its rule over a vast territory prone to sporadic rebellions. Demographic changes, including large-scale conversions, altered the profile of the empire's population and resulted in both an increasingly non-Arab administrative elite and a pro-Arab backlash. The conversion of non-Arabs to Islam and their integration into elite Muslim institutions such as the army, scholarly circles, and especially the caliphal court posed political and ideological challenges. Iranian and other converts gained prominence in the court hierarchy and the specialized religious sciences, challenging Arab supremacy. This resulted in the so-called Shu'ubiyya movement. The secretarial class associated with the Abbasid government had arrogated power to itself and adopted some of the trappings of the Sassanian empire. The increased prominence of converts and clients meant that Arabs were not automatically granted the social prestige that had been theirs during Umayyad rule. Both Arabs and more recent converts were among the scholars who flourished under caliphal patronage. Rulers supported both natural sciences and religious disciplines, including philosophy and theology. One theological tendency, Mu'tazilism, grew into a force to be reckoned with. I will have more to say about it a bit later.

Even as scholarship thrived, political turmoil simmered. Despite the theoretical existence of a unified (Sunni) caliphate from Abu Bakr's accession at the Prophet's death in 23/632 until the early twentieth-century abolition of the office under the Ottomans, fragmentation and instability were more often than not the order of the day. The repeated uprisings, rebellions, and political shifts of early Islamic history colored Shafi'i's environment.

The question of legitimate leadership had led to the first intra-Muslim conflict, over the succession to the caliphate. Some, eventually known as Shi'a, advocated the leadership of 'Ali. 'Alid partisanship came in numerous gradations. An extremist minority came to consider 'Ali more important than Muhammad. A larger group advocated the right of 'Ali and his descendants to govern, including some who thought that he alone of the early caliphs was acceptable. Shafi'i was not among those who saw all non-'Alid rulers as illegitimate. Instead, he was part of a much larger group that saw in 'Ali and his progeny special merit as members of the Prophet's household. What we know of his allegiances suggests both an acceptance of the legitimacy of the first four caliphs (his reported ranking of their merit falls conveniently into line with later Sunni orthodoxy) and a particular attachment to 'Ali as a member of the Prophet's household. Of course, there is a tension between the two. One of his students testifies: "I heard Shafi'i say about excellence: Abu Bakr, and 'Umar, and 'Uthman, and 'Ali." Another declaration makes Shafi'i's views on these men's respective merit even more explicit: "He said, 'After God's Messenger, peace be upon him, the most excellent of people is Abu Bakr, then 'Umar, then 'Uthman, then 'Ali, may God be pleased with all of them" (B 432–3). Even as Shafi'i trumpets his attachment to the Prophet's household in his poetry, he denies it political significance. In a poem entitled "His love for the people of the house," he confesses his love for the Prophet's family while implicitly denying that this constitutes Rafidism, the view that 'Ali was most entitled to the caliphate:

> If Rafidism is love for Muhammad's family
> Then let both humans and jinn testify that I am a Rafidi.
>
> *(Diwan 55)*

Centuries later, a similar couplet by the South Arabian 'Abd al-Qadir al-'Aydarus (d. 1037/1628) echoes Shafi'i's combination of declared affection for the members of the Prophet's household and grandstanding defensiveness about its implications:

> I love the Prophet Muhammad and his family:
> If that makes me a Shi'ite, that's fine with me.
>
> *(al-'Aydarus 2001, 213)*

Ibn al-Nadim, author of the *Fihrist* – a medieval bookseller's catalogue that has become an invaluable resource for intellectual historians – refers to Shafi'i as "strongly partisan" or "strongly Shi'i" (*shadid fi'l-tashayyu'*). His assessment is both frequently repeated and generally discounted. It raises a larger question, though, about gradations of reverence. How does one move from love for the people of the house to partisanship or at the very least sympathy for 'Alid rebels? Here, two questions arise. The first has to do with 'Alid leanings and the second with the authority of the state and the legitimacy of rebellion.

Shafi'i's penchant for 'Alid causes had precedent among the legal classes. Neither the Umayyads nor the Abbasids shared the prestige attached to those men immediately surrounding Muhammad. Contests over legitimate rule, of course, were not limited to those involving 'Alids but many of the rebellions, especially in the provinces, supported one or another of 'Ali's descendants and there was a precedent for supporting 'Alid contenders among Sunni scholars. Abu Hanifa is said to have supported the anti-Umayyad rebel Zayd ibn 'Ali, who was executed in 122/740; more problematically, his expressed support for the 145/762 Medinan rebellion of another 'Alid, Muhammad ibn 'Abdallah, known as "the pure soul" (al-Nafs al-Zakiyya), may have provoked his imprisonment by the caliph. Malik did not join this latter rebellion but apparently opined that it was permissible for others to pledge their allegiance to the rebel. Shafi'i was not inherently opposed to supporting a rebel: he declared, according to his student Harmala ibn Yahya (d. 243/857), that it was legitimate to fight alongside and pray behind anyone who proclaimed himself caliph after attaining military victory and gaining the backing of the populace. This was a pragmatic rather than ideological assessment: he pointed out that anyone who failed to win battles or popular support was merely sowing dissension.

YEMEN AND YAHYA IBN 'ABDALLAH

We are now slightly better positioned to evaluate the conflicting reports about Shafi'i's participation in an 'Alid rebellion against the

Abbasid caliphs. At the end of the second/eighth century, Yemen was a volatile backwater, distant from major trade routes and prone to periodic outbreaks of rebellion, sometimes by tribes, sometimes by 'Alid pretenders to the caliphate, who asserted the illegitimacy of the Sunni central government and the right of 'Ali's descendants to rule. The monumental *History of Prophets and Kings* of Tabari (d. 310/923) details aspects of Abbasid political and court life; stretches catalogue one 'Alid uprising after another. Because of this instability, governors were dispatched from Iraq to represent the regime. For a while, one governor was set over the Hijaz and Yemen together. At the time Shafi'i went, independent governors for Yemen were being sent directly from Baghdad.

It is probable that Shafi'i, now in his early thirties, served in Najran as deputy to the governor appointed by Harun al-Rashid. Less certain is the consequence that some describe: something went wrong and Shafi'i got arrested. One version has it, vaguely, that the governor oppressed the Yemeni populace. Shafi'i intervened in the service of justice – with the scholar's weapon, words – and earned the governor's ire. The governor tattled to the caliph, casting aspersions on Shafi'i's loyalty to the regime. More serious accusations involve his collusion – real or fabricated by jealous enemies – in a rebellion by Yahya ibn 'Abdallah, a descendant of 'Ali ibn Abi Talib's son Hasan. (Some of Yahya's biographers say Shafi'i studied with him in Sana'a in the mid 170s/790s when Shafi'i was likely still in Medina.) Though these accounts disagree as to whether he merely sympathized with Yahya or formally pledged allegiance to him, all agree that Shafi'i never took up arms. Nevertheless, he was arrested with a group of nine Shi'i partisans in Yemen – or, in a variant, in Mecca with a group of Quraysh who had rallied behind the Yemeni rebel – and brought to Iraq to face the caliph. Most reports place this encounter in 187 or 189, although Muhammad Abu Zahra sets it in 184. (Yahya ibn 'Abdallah probably died in prison in 187/803.) Still others, quite reasonably, believe the whole thing is a fabrication.

Shafi'i's capture and confrontation with the caliph is a good story and it could be true; rulers arrested, interrogated, and punished scholars for infractions actual and imagined. And yet, as with other elements of scholarly biographies such as amazing feats of memory or dream-visions where the Prophet verifies the soundness of a particular teacher's approach, Shafi'i getting dragged before the caliph echoes numerous similar tales and serves literary purposes quite apart from any consideration of whether it is factually accurate. Apart from adding drama, the encounter where he wins his freedom while the (other) conspirators are executed highlights Shafi'i's quick thinking alongside his political-religious loyalties. In some tellings, Shafi'i's compelling speech and persuasive arguments carry the day. In one version, Shafi'i addresses al-Rashid casually, omitting all usual honorifics. Questioned about his presumption, he appeals to their shared kinship and, by extension, their shared kinship with the Prophet. Cousins, after all, need not be formal with one another. He distances himself from the rebels in another account by appealing to tribal heritage to explain why he supports al-Rashid. The 'Alids think of others as their slaves, but the Abbasids view Shafi'i's clan as their brothers. Once again, lineage matters.

Most biographers proffer an alternate or additional explanation for Shafi'i's acquittal: Shaybani's intervention. Shaybani, once student to Malik and Abu Hanifa, would become a crucial figure in Shafi'i's intellectual trajectory. Legal historian Joseph Schacht (1953), who accepts that Shafi'i went to Yemen but doubts his involvement with a sectarian uprising, suggests that the encounter with Harun al-Rashid functions as a narrative device to introduce Shaybani to the plot of Shafi'i's life. Éric Chaumont (2006), on the other hand, accepts the caliphal audience and sees Shaybani's involvement as more plausible than the "hagiographic version" where Shafi'i's own eloquence carries the day. Traditional Muslim biographers differ over details but accept the story in its basic outlines, complete with triumphal pardon: the other conspirators are executed and Shafi'i is released with the caliph's admiration, and a massive reward of 50,000 dirhams or 5000 dinars.

THE IRAQI LEGAL SCENE

Released from prison and newly flush or, if one rejects the story of the caliphal audience, recently arrived from Yemen or the Hijaz under his own steam to continue his legal studies, Shafi'i began to interact, discuss, and argue with Iraqi scholarly authorities and younger scholars. Baghdad was, as far as sources allow us to deduce, where Shafi'i spent most of his time in Iraq, though his writings mention visits to Kufa, which had long been the center of the Iraqi legal scene. Abu Hanifa's circle was based there, as were earlier authorities on whom he drew, such as Ibrahim al-Nakha'i (d. ca. 96/717) and Hammad ibn Abi Sulayman (d. 120/738). Disputation and disagreement figured prominently, and teaching was characterized by a dialogical format. "What if?" and "Do you not see?" peppered lectures and conversations. Systematic thinking was increasingly valued but Abu Hanifa also cited the precedent of his own teachers as authoritative, as well as, when the occasion called for it, the views or precedents of Muhammad and especially his Companions, a number of whom had settled in Kufa.

Abu Hanifa died in Baghdad in 150/767, the year of Shafi'i's birth, possibly poisoned, or under torture, or in prison. Some report that his fall was a consequence of refusing the caliph al-Mansur's offer of a judgeship. As political appointments, judgeships carried the benefits and risks inherent in patronage positions. Manuals for the conduct of legal scholars routinely counsel the rejection of judgeships, since one incurs the responsibility of judging fairly, the weight of expectations, and the temptations of both lucre and power. One must not judge in anger, nor allow personal feelings to color one's judgment, and of course one must refuse bribes. Chronicles and biographical dictionaries list men who refused the position of judge or who, in such a role, turned away those who would influence their rulings through graft. Nonetheless, not everyone refused, whether because of pressures brought to bear by rulers to accept or because they considered the risks to be outweighed by the social and economic benefits associated with the role. Abu Yusuf Ya'qub (d. 182/798), also a Kufan, who took over Abu Hanifa's circle when the latter died, had a long career as a judge in Baghdad. He was often called Abu Yusuf the Judge and was the first to be honored with the title of chief judge (*qadi al-qudat*).

Abu Yusuf inherited Abu Hanifa's students along with his circle, including Shaybani. Born in Wasit in 132/750 and brought up in Kufa, Shaybani had begun study with Abu Hanifa at age fourteen or sixteen. When Abu Hanifa died a few years later, Shaybani continued his studies with Abu Yusuf for a time before traveling to Medina to study with Malik. Shaybani reportedly spent three years with Malik and heard hundreds of hadith from him. He then returned to Iraq, where he used what he had learned from Malik to bolster, and sometimes modify, Abu Hanifa's views.

We owe the bulk of early Hanafi texts to Shaybani or those writing in his name. (A few works attributed to Abu Yusuf survive, including the *Disagreements between Abu Hanifa and Ibn Abi Layla*, which Shafi'i transmitted, with his own commentary, as *Disagreements between the Two Iraqis*.) In addition to works of positive law, two works compare the teachings of Malik and Abu Hanifa. The *Muwatta' Shaybani* is a recension of Malik's *Muwatta'* with commentary describing Abu Hanifa's positions on the matters in question. Shaybani mostly champions Abu Hanifa's views, but in a significant minority of cases he adopts Malik's position, most often when Abu Hanifa seems to ignore a direct prophetic precedent. For instance, he agrees with Malik that a male guardian must contract a woman's marriage, citing a hadith to that effect.

Where the *Muwatta' Shaybani* seeks primarily to compare and explain, the second work, the *Kitab al-Hujja* or *Book of Refutation of the People of Medina*, argues vigorously, sometimes viciously against the Medinans of whom Malik is the prime representative. Unlike in the *Muwatta' Shaybani*, where Shaybani occasionally sides with the Medinans, the *Hujja*, though deeply familiar with Medinan doctrines, is purely a defense of Abu Hanifa's views; on the subject of women concluding their own marriage contracts, for example, the *Hujja* is strictly in favor.

After serving, perhaps reluctantly, as a judge in Raqqa (ca. 180–7/796–803), Shaybani was dismissed from his post in 187/803. The reason remains murky, but it may have been his stance on a safe passage pledge extended by the caliph to the rebel Yahya ibn 'Abdallah a decade earlier and which the caliph wanted, illegitimately in Shaybani's view, to revoke. (Shaybani's locking horns with the caliph on this safe conduct pass is far better attested than any stories about Shafi'i's involvement with the same rebel.) Shaybani returned to Baghdad, and Chaumont suggests that this was when Shafi'i studied with him. Shafi'i's biographers usually place his journey to Iraq slightly earlier, around 184, and often suggest that he returned to Mecca around 186. Here we confront another of the intractable problems of chronology that crop up in Shafi'i's story. Without any firm dates to pin down the period between his childhood memorization of the Qur'an and his arrival in Egypt when he was nearing fifty, any narrative must be provisional.

At some point Shafi'i married, probably in Mecca but possibly while in Sana'a, Yemen. His bride was Qurashi, descended from the third caliph 'Uthman. Known as "the 'Uthmaniyya," Hamida (or possibly Hamda or Jamila – the Arabic script looks very similar) bint Nafi' ibn 'Anbasa (or 'Uyayna) ibn 'Amr ibn 'Uthman ibn 'Affan eventually bore him three children. The first, a son named Muhammad and known as Abu 'Uthman, became a judge in Aleppo and died sometime after 240/854. The second and third were daughters, named Fatima and Zaynab after two of the Prophet's daughters. (While in Egypt, Shafi'i also had a son by a slave concubine; I will say more about them later. An isolated account suggests that he married again after this child's birth, the year before he died. He divorced this wife, Zuhriya, the daughter of Abu Zurara al-Zuhri, after consummating the marriage. Presumably there were no children from the union.) His will shows that Hamida and their children settled in Mecca, where Shafi'i maintained close connections with his extended natal family. There is no indication that his family was with him in Iraq, and some evidence to suggest that they were in Mecca for much of this time.

Shafi'i, now in his mid-to-late thirties, spent part of the second half of the 180s/800s in Iraq, pursuing knowledge of various kinds. One teacher in hadith was 'Abd al-Wahhab ibn 'Abd al-Majid al-Thaqafi (d. 194/809) who also taught Ahmad ibn Hanbal (d. 241/855); Shafi'i relates hadith on al-Thaqafi's authority in his *Umm*. He obtained some grammatical knowledge; many of the technical terms he uses in his works on legal method are adapted from grammar. He was also undoubtedly exposed to the currents of theological thinking that flourished in Iraq at the time. It seems unlikely that he had no interest: Shafi'i was interested in everything. On the other hand, it seems even less likely that he pursued formal study of theology. Even if one distrusts the biographical sources, which are intent on painting him as one who rejects theological controversy, it seems clear that his theological vision is too tightly wedded to his vision of revealed law to leave room for broader speculation.

The most crucial element of this period in Iraq, of course, was his study and engagement with Abu Hanifa's disciple Shaybani. His influence on Shafi'i's thinking was probably accomplished through some combination of writings and direct encounters. Shafi'i affirms having paid 50 or 60 dinars for Shaybani's books, or, in another version, having copied them himself. "I copied the books of Muhammad ibn al-Hasan [Shaybani] and knew his views" (IAH 160). We know little of their personal interaction, though Shafi'i reportedly said "I have never seen a heavy man as lighthearted as Muhammad ibn al-Hasan, nor anyone more eloquent than him" (IAH 132).

Shafi'i's engagement with Shaybani included debate and argument with him, his disciples, and other local figures. In these debates, the sources say that Shaybani championed Abu Hanifa while Shafi'i enacted the role of Malik's follower, albeit an increasingly independent one. (When he cannot entirely squash claims attributing a particularly objectionable position to Shafi'i, the biographer Ahmad ibn Husayn al-Bayhaqi [d. 458/1066] resorts to suggesting that Shafi'i may have made the statement in a debate with Shaybani as a concession regarding the Medinan position on the matter – not his own.) These stories, however, likely exaggerate the parity between the men: it would be some time before Shafi'i would stand on his own as a legal thinker.

Engagement with Shaybani made him familiar with – even if he chose not to adopt – many Hanafi positions, though Shafi'i's treatment of Abu Hanifa's positions is usually less detailed and less confident than his treatment of Malik's views. It also honed Shafi'i's skills in both oral and written disputation. One of the most telling facts about Shafi'i's development as a thinker, as well as the legal climate of the times, is that he wrote a *Refutation of Muhammad ibn al-Hasan [Shaybani]*.

2

FROM STUDENT TO SHAYKH

In the wake of his time with Shaybani and other Iraqi scholars, Shafi'i probably returned to Mecca in the late 180s or early 190s (perhaps around 805 CE). Numerous reports describe him leading a teaching circle in Mecca's main mosque in the area surrounding the Ka'ba and lecturing occasionally after Friday prayers. He ruminated on methodological inconsistencies that niggled at him. The weaknesses of Malik's teachings had become apparent during his study and debate in Iraq; simple appeals to Medinan practice and to the authority of local jurists were untenable in the face of Iraqi demands for logical coherence. Yet the flaws of the Iraqi approaches – the inconstant nature of legal positions, and a seeming disregard for authoritative precedent – were equally unpalatable. Shafi'i began to formulate independent doctrines and to focus on method. The content of his ideas would grow and change over the three stages Abu Zahra identifies in his teaching career: in Mecca, Baghdad (in a second visit), and Egypt.

Among those who sat in Shafi'i's Meccan circle was Ibn Hanbal, who might have also learned from him in Baghdad. It is impossible to gauge how well the two really knew each other or what Ibn Hanbal's impressions of Shafi'i might have been but tracking the pendulum-swing between admiration and suspicion of Shafi'i's legal acumen can help us understand how the two men came to personify overlapping trends in the development of law.

Both Ibn Hanbal and Shafi'i "integrated traditions [consistently] into their jurisprudence" (Spectorsky 2002, 74), but this similarity should not obscure important differences. Where Shafi'i's concerns revolved around consistency, non-contradiction, and the method governing the legal use of hadith, Ibn Hanbal cared little for the integration of hadith into a larger pattern, or for resolving seeming contradictions between them. Unlike Shafi'i, Ibn Hanbal was willing to leave matters unresolved if there were conflicting hadith of equal value, or suspend judgment if there was no hadith on the subject. The biggest difference between the two men, though, was not in their theoretical approach to tradition but in their relationship to it. Ibn Hanbal was, above all, a traditionist (that is, someone who reports hadith or traditions). His best known work is his *Musnad*, a collection of hadith, not his collected responsa, treatises recording his answers to legal queries posed to him. By contrast, although his jurisprudence relied heavily on hadith, usually if not always reported with chains of transmission as he heard them from his teachers, Shafi'i was thoroughly a jurist.

Anecdotes that record Ibn Hanbal's positive impressions of Shafi'i distinguish between Shafi'i's clear fields of expertise – jurisprudence and reasoning – and Ibn Hanbal's own specialization in hadith-study. One account suggests that he accepted Shafi'i's dicta in the absence of sound hadith on a particular issue. Another report says that Ibn Hanbal chose to sit in Shafi'i's circle rather than that of Sufyan ibn 'Uyayna, a teacher they had shared. Questioned as to why he would choose to listen to someone whose age was so close to his in preference to a senior instructor, Ibn Hanbal defended his choice based on Shafi'i's unique qualifications; by contrast, he points out that hadith transmitters are interchangeable, since one can always hear the same hadith with a longer chain of transmitters. These anecdotes portray Ibn Hanbal admiring Shafi'i's grasp of jurisprudential reasoning but harboring deep suspicions of both analogy and the practice of entertaining hypothetical questions. Shafi'i is portrayed as adept at solving logical conundrums: "Shafi'i was asked about a man who had a date in his mouth, and said: If I eat it, my wife is divorced, and if I spit it out, my wife is divorced. He said: He eats half of it, and spits out half" (Ibn Qadi Shubha 2003, 43). Ibn Hanbal, on the other hand, displays reticence in speculating about situations of this sort, and sometimes demurs ("I am afraid to answer") in response to queries which call for extrapolation.

Ishaq ibn Rahawayh (d. 238/853), who sometimes traveled with Ibn Hanbal, had no such qualms about Shafi'i's jurisprudential bent. He attended Shafi'i's teaching circle in Mecca and later copied his writings for himself. Originally from Merv, he also reportedly studied, like Shafi'i and Ibn Hanbal, with Sufyan ibn 'Uyayna. He eventually settled in Nishapur. There, he may have borrowed Shafi'i's writings from the Nishapuri hadith scholar Tirmidhi. A more fanciful explanation shows Ibn Rahawayh going to extraordinary lengths to gain access to these works: he married a widow in Merv just because her late husband had possessed copies of Shafi'i's writings. The different accounts as to how he got these writings suggest doubt that Ibn Rahawayh attended Shafi'i's lectures for any protracted period.

This array of anecdotes reporting interactions between Shafi'i and Ibn Hanbal is fairly typical. They show that Ibn Hanbal and Shafi'i likely met and interacted; they reveal the importance later biographers placed on these interactions and the rhetorical uses they made of them. Shafi'i serves as the linchpin of the four imams. Having studied with Malik and Abu Hanifa's major disciple (and let us not forget the tentative link between Shafi'i's birth and Abu Hanifa's death), it remains only to connect him to Ibn Hanbal for there to be a perfect square. Of the four, Ibn Hanbal was least interested in systematization and "law-making." Shafi'i's sympathies lay with the partisans of hadith but he was a jurist. His sensibilities about prophetic sunna and the importance of properly transmitted hadith served as a means to criticize the juristic circles of his time. He wielded jurisprudence in the service of tradition rather than as a substitute for it. In so doing he also cemented the inadequacy of hadith scholarship as a path to religious law.

BACK TO IRAQ

Probably around 195/810, now in his mid-forties, Shafi'i returned to Baghdad with an established reputation and taught for a stint. He should probably no longer be considered a follower of Malik, though there had been no definitive break. Yet he had not moved closer to Iraqi jurisprudence. If anything, his objections to the methods of Shaybani and Abu Yusuf had hardened and a notable feature of his teaching was opposition to the dominant strands of thinking in Iraq.

His teaching circle started small. One account says he had half a dozen companions on his arrival. Eventually his followers increased to the point that he had to move his circle to the Great Mosque. Al-Khatib al-Baghdadi (d. 463/1071) tells us, implausibly, in his history of Baghdad that Shafi'i's circle took up the entire space, which had previously accommodated forty or fifty circles. A slightly less grandiose account says that as his circle grew, the circles of the partisans of opinion diminished from twenty to three or four.

During this second Iraqi period, he apparently composed a work of substantive law called the *Hujja* (*Proof* or possibly *Refutation*), which has not survived. Some of its substantive doctrines, known as his "old" teaching, are attested in a variety of places, including in transmissions by a handful of students who studied with him in Mecca and/or Baghdad. In addition to Ibn Hanbal, who reportedly studied with him in both cities, three figures are well known: Abu Thawr (d. 240/854), Al-Husayn al-Karabisi (d. 245/859 or 248/862–3), and Al-Hasan ibn Muhammad al-Za'farani (d. 260/874). Abu Thawr, a Baghdadi, was a former adherent of Iraqi reasoning but when Shafi'i came to Baghdad – presumably in the 190s – Abu Thawr discarded opinion for hadith. Al-Khatib al-Baghdadi credits Abu Thawr with a book of rulings combining hadith and jurisprudence. He transmitted Shafi'i's old doctrine but also had an independent school. Though it became defunct, writing in the fourth/tenth century the bookseller Ibn al-Nadim noted its prevalence in Azerbaijan and Armenia (Dodge 1970, 520). Karabisi was, like Abu Thawr, a convert from Iraqi modes of jurisprudence who transmitted Shafi'i's old doctrine. He portrays Shafi'i as the reason he and others gave up reliance on the writings of the Iraqis, abandoning innovation (*bid'a*) in favor of reliance on sunna as Shafi'i defined it. He was perhaps the most important of Shafi'i's Iraqi students, but eventually became associated with debate over the creation of the Qur'an. Za'farani, who avoided entanglement in theological controversies, is variously depicted as having transmitted Shafi'i's views faithfully and reliably and, alternately, as having modified what he heard.

Abu 'Abd al-Rahman al-Shafi'i (fl. 219/834, d. after 230/845), otherwise jurisprudentially undistinguished as Shafi'i's student (and considered theologically suspect by later members of the school), later taught Dawud ibn Khalaf (d. 270/883–4), better known as Dawud al-Zahiri (Dawud the Literalist). Dawud, who never met Shafi'i, was the founder of his own rationalist school of jurisprudence, the Zahiris, whose best-known member is the fifth/eleventh-century Andalusian jurist Ibn Hazm. Though the school faded, the Zahiris' extreme positions made them appealing targets for various arguments in works of legal theory over the centuries. Dawud was also the author of an early work in praise of Shafi'i, excerpted in al-Khatib al-Baghdadi's *History*. The connection between the two innovative legal thinkers makes sense given their similarities of temperament. Even though Dawud rejected the possibility of analogical reasoning, one of the key tenets of Shafi'i's system, one suspects they were kindred spirits, fully committed to carrying their logical presuppositions through to their ends.

INTO EGYPT

The rudiments of Shafi'i's legal theory were by now in place. Certain characteristic ideas as well as specific doctrines were already associated with him, such as the importance of hadith and the significance of Muhammad's precedent. A final coherent statement of his methodological views would emerge in Egypt, where he is said to have changed his mind on certain substantive doctrines and perhaps become more uncompromising on certain matters of method, including an unsparing critique of Malik's legal approach.

There is disagreement about precisely when Shafi'i's stay in Egypt began. Some posit two periods there, interrupted by a few years in Iraq. The first would have begun in approximately 188–9/804 and the second in 198/814 or slightly later. But, as Jonathan Brockopp points out, Shafi'i does not seem to have interacted with several key Maliki figures (Ibn Wahb [197/813], Ibn al-Qasim [d. 191/806], and Sahnun ibn Sa'id al-Tanukhi [d. 240/854]) who were in Egypt in the late 180s and early 190s (about 804–11). Thus, it seems reasonable to conclude that Shafi'i moved there only when approaching his fiftieth year, arriving from Mecca (or possibly Iraq) in 198/814 or thereabouts. Though the sources do not permit certainty, I think it probable that Shafi'i was living in Mecca before he moved to Egypt. One can explain the visit to Baghdad in 198/814 that some biographers report: he may have left Egypt shortly after arriving due to a sudden souring of the political climate, sojourning in Baghdad for a few months.

The political context matters because, according to the historian al-Kindi (d. 350/961), Shafi'i had arrived in Egypt in 198/814 attached to an Abbasid figure whose rule ended up being controversial. Shafi'i accompanied 'Abdallah, son (and possibly deputy) of the new Baghdad-appointed governor al-'Abbas ibn Musa. Al-'Abbas's governorship failed quickly; after several strife-filled years, the Khurasani al-Sari ibn al-Hakam acceded to the role, which he held for the rest of Shafi'i's life.

Apart from the Abbasid tie, there is speculation about why Shafi'i moved to Egypt. One explanation is that he refused a judgeship and had to clear out of town. Chaumont hypothesizes more prosaically that the strength of Malik's disciples in the Hijaz had induced Shafi'i to leave for Iraq, while the dominance of Shaybani's acolytes in Baghdad eventually prompted Shafi'i's move to Egypt. But Egypt was full of wealthy and influential Malikis; if he were seeking to escape their sphere, Egypt would not have been a likely destination. Shafi'i had a tie to a prominent Maliki family, the 'Abd al-Hakam clan. He might have met Ibn 'Abd al-Hakam, who would later author a compendium of Maliki jurisprudence, while studying in the Hijaz. Both men had studied with Sufyan ibn 'Uyayna and Muslim ibn Khalid al-Zanji in Mecca, as well as Malik in Medina. Ibn 'Abd al-Hakam was instrumental in getting Shafi'i settled in Egypt; in addition to hosting him when he first arrived, he borrowed money or stood surety for a loan of 3000 dinars to get Shafi'i established. It is possible that his host did not realize the extent to which he had strayed from Malik's doctrines during the intervening years. In Iraq, Shafi'i had directed most of his criticisms against the doctrines prevalent there (though he certainly did not spare Malik's views); perhaps it was his re-entry into a Maliki-dominated space that led him to formulate and broadcast his decisive criticisms of Malik's method.

The intense and long-lasting engagement of Shafi'i with Malik, his ideas, and followers, makes any attempt firmly to separate a Maliki from a Shafi'i school during Shafi'i's lifetime, or even that of his immediate followers, suspect. The boundaries between groups of jurists were still porous. The relatively fluid nature of scholarly allegiances, though, did not make conflicts less meaningful. Rivalries between camps of jurists, usually waged through public disputations, sometimes devolved into less refined tactics. Shafi'i, who had once identified as a disciple of Malik, had begun to approach specific legal queries by appealing to an overarching or undergirding structure that could address questions of evidence and proof. The impetus to think about these issues systematically led him to a test out his legal-theoretical ideas in conversations, lessons, and perhaps a draft of what would become the *Risala*. And in that work, as well as in his lessons, he increasingly argued against key features of Malik's legal method, especially his reliance on the communal precedent of Medina.

THE SHAFI'I SCHOOL

Shafi'i lectured daily in the main mosque of Fustat (Old Cairo), which was named for 'Amr ibn al-'As, Egypt's conqueror, who established Fustat as a garrison town. The mosque, much expanded, still stands today, though the head of the rebel Zayd ibn 'Ali, once displayed on its pulpit, was removed even before Shafi'i's time. Although Shafi'i is sometimes said to have given lessons in several disciplines, including hadith, theology, poetry, and Qur'anic interpretation, and to have attracted audiences of up to 300 people, we may take some of this as exaggeration. In any case, it is as a jurist that his teachings were most significant. Those teachings were the basis for the *Umm*, a restatement and updating of the *Hujja* composed in Iraq.

Out of the larger group of those who attended his teaching circle, around a half dozen men became prominent disciples and are listed as transmitters of Shafi'i's "new" doctrines. Harmala ibn Yahya, sometimes referred to as Abu Hafs, and Yunus ibn 'Abd al-A'la (d. 264/879), sometimes called Abu Musa, are cited as authorities for numerous biographical anecdotes about Shafi'i. Ibn 'Abd al-Hakam's son Muhammad ibn 'Abdallah (d. 268/882) appears in some lists. He attended Shafi'i's teaching circle assiduously. For a time one of Shafi'i's most favored students – he is said to have breakfasted with the teacher frequently – Muhammad ibn 'Abdallah later disavowed Shafi'i's teachings and rejoined the Malikis after Shafi'i's death, though this may have been sour grapes resulting from infighting about succession within his circle. He also wrote a *Refutation of Shafi'i* proclaiming Shafi'i's deviation from Qur'an and sunna. In this, he was following in the footsteps of Shafi'i, whose refutations of both Malik and Shaybani are preserved in works designed to point out *their* divergences from scripture.

The Meccan 'Abdallah ibn al-Zubayr al-Humaydi (d. 219/834) studied with Sufyan ibn 'Uyayna and Shafi'i in Mecca before continuing his studies with the latter in Egypt. He returned to Mecca after Shafi'i died, though some accounts suggest that he stayed around long enough to wrangle over leadership of Shafi'i's circle. Three men, however, were most important: Rabi' ibn Sulayman al-Muradi, Abu Ya'qub al-Buwayti (d. 231/846), and Isma'il ibn Yahya al-Muzani (d. 264/877–8). Rabi', Buwayti, and Muzani are essential to the narrative of Shafi'ism after the master's death. Shafi'i reportedly called Buwayti "my tongue," Muzani "the one who made my method (or doctrine) triumph" (*nasir madhhabi*), and Rabi' "the transmitter of my writings" (*rawiyat kutubi*)." These characterizations amount to a tripartite division between the school, the method ("the *madhhab*" – not in its later sense of legal school but rather as a mode of doing jurisprudence), and the writings.

There is some confusion as to the first of these men, since two Rabi's figure in some lists of Shafi'i's disciples, one important and one peripheral. Rabi' ibn Sulayman al-Jizi (d. 256/870) was "fairly insignificant in all respects" (Melchert 1997, 81) and Kevin Jaques (2007) has recently suggested that he was not a Shafi'i at all, but rather a Maliki dragged into the narrative of the early Shafi'i school to preserve the reputation of Rabi' ibn Sulayman al-Muradi as faithful transmitter of Shafi'i's works: any suggestion of criticism or deviation attributed to Muradi could be fobbed off on Jizi. The eighth/fourteenth-century scholar al-Dhahabi conflates the two Rabi's into Rabi' ibn Sulayman al-Muradi al-Jizi.

Rabi' ibn Sulayman al-Muradi (hereafter, simply Rabi') is an absolutely essential part of Shafi'ism's history. He and Shafi'i apparently met at the congregational mosque in Fustat, where he eventually worked as a *muezzin*. (Shafi'i may have obtained this job for him in 201/816–17, when Rabi' married.) He played a fundamental role in the recording, shaping, and passing down of Shafi'i's works, especially the *Umm*, by compiling and teaching them. He taught dozens of students. A certain Abu Zur'a reports having heard Shafi'i's writings from Rabi' in 228/842–3: Rabi' read them out loud to him. He sold two garments for funds to buy the paper (which had begun to replace papyrus in Egypt) to make copies for himself. Rabi' likely composed *Disagreements between Malik and Shafi'i*. It is unclear to what extent Rabi' merits his reputation as somewhat dim; he was appointed under the governorship of Ibn Tulun (r. 254–70/868–84) to teach in the new major mosque, which makes it unlikely he was as dumb as the sources sometimes make him out to be. Still, there is no reason to suspect that he had the kind of incisive, creative legal mind that characterized Muzani.

"From the juridical point of view Muzani was by far the most important" of Shafi'i's disciples (Melchert 2004, 80). Like Abu Thawr among Shafi'i's Baghdadi students, Muzani was an independent thinker. He is generally said to be a former Hanafi, though what precisely this means is uncertain. The prominent Hanafi Abu Ja'far al-Tahawi (d. 321/933) was his nephew as well as, for a time, his student. Muzani taught numerous others, but his most important contribution was his *Mukhtasar* or *Digest*, which became a vital text for the teaching and learning of Shafi'i jurisprudence. He hews fairly closely to Shafi'i's doctrines in most respects, but on several occasions he points out seeming errors in logic and chooses to depart from Shafi'i's views. At other times, he promotes what he sees as the master's legal principles over and against specific rules.

Where Rabi' passed on Shafi'i's texts, Muzani passed along a set of legal techniques. He developed Shafi'i's work on prohibitions into a more sophisticated theory of commands and prohibitions. Muzani's methods-focused approach to Shafi'i's jurisprudence came to dominate. It could, however, have gone differently had Buwayti's traditionalist Shafi'ism won the day as it briefly seemed likely to do. While Muzani stresses analogy and the extraction of general guiding principles by which to judge individual cases, Buwayti minimizes analogy, emphasizes hadith, and displays – perhaps not surprisingly given Buwayti's Maliki past – "a distinctly conciliatory attitude towards Malikism" (El Shamsy 2009, 182). Although in some respects the Shafi'i school took a more strongly rationalist turn, Buwayti's traditionalist credentials, along with those of Humaydi, helped Shafi'i's methodological ideals spread to those affiliated with other emergent schools and those in Ibn Hanbal's "traditionist-jurisprudent" camp.

The epithet "my tongue" gives Shafi'i's imprimatur to Buwayti's leadership. It is almost certainly, therefore, not a genuine utterance but part of a partisan arsenal deployed by Buwayti's supporters in the wake of Shafi'i's death, or subsequent scholars looking to retrospectively justify the school's direction. It finds further expression in Ibn Qadi Shubha's entry for Buwayti in his biographical dictionary of Shafi'i jurists. Shafi'i, he writes, designated Buwayti to lead his circle after him, and said "There is no one with more right to my assembly (*majlis*) than Abu Ya'qub [Buwayti], and there is no one among my companions more knowledgeable than him." He quotes prominent figures affirming Buwayti's superiority over both Muzani and Rabi' and claims that Buwayti's versions of Shafi'i's books have the fewest mistakes. Subki (1999, 1:383–9) simply calls him "the greatest of Shafi'i's followers."

CONFLICT AND CONFRONTATION

I have gotten ahead of myself by discussing the posthumous organization of Shafi'i's school. I now return to events which some sources say precipitated his death. His public criticisms of Malik's teachings made his relationship with the Egyptian Maliki elite volatile. As his prestige grew, some powerful Malikis complained to government officials, seeking to have him banished or chastised. One prominent Maliki, Fityan ibn Abi Samh (d. 232/846–7), attacked Shafi'i and was punished by the governor. El Shamsy (2009, 113–14) summarizes the affair:

> In the course of an impassioned debate between Fityan and Shafi'i, the former appears to have uttered something ... that could have been construed as an insult to the Prophet Muhammad. When word of Fityan's statement reached al-Sari ibn al-Hakam, he sentenced Fityan to public whipping as punishment for the affront to the Prophet. This incident, involving as it did a prominent and respected member of the Egyptian elite, led to a violent public outburst against Shafi'i, who was subsequently attacked by a mob and thereafter confined to his house until his death – for how long is not known. That the incident did not simply reflect a personal conflict between Shafi'i and Fityan is

indicated by the fact that both Ashhab and 'Isa ibn al-Munkadir are reported to have prayed in public for Shafi'i's death. 'Isa is quoted as having said to Shafi'i, "O you nothing, when you came to our country, we were united and our doctrine was one; but then you sowed division and spread evil, so may God separate your body and soul!"

Ashhab (d. 204/819), who died at most a few months before Shafi'i, is said elsewhere to have "cursed Shafi'i from his deathbed" (Brockopp 2000, 206).

The whole story seems unnecessarily dramatic. Shafi'i's death was more likely the result of a lingering illness, possibly a recurring stomach complaint, than injury by an impassioned mob. After all, he did draft a will the previous year, though this could have been prompted by the desire to settle affairs for his newly born son. The precise contours of the dispute, too, seem contrived, though scholarly debates could spark rioting. Crowd violence could funnel through allegiance to legal schools, which were increasingly also social movements, with large groups of lay adherents as well as small numbers of scholar-practitioners. (Several decades later, Iraqi Hanbalis would engage regularly in street brawls.)

Even if he was persecuted by disaffected Malikis, the climate of generalized acrimony did not destroy the friendship between him and the 'Abd al-Hakam family. Their connection remained close despite their parting of the ways in legal matters. Muhammad ibn 'Abdallah, the son of Ibn 'Abd al-Hakam, expressed his deep respect and affection for Shafi'i despite their differences: "There is no one among those who disagree with us [i.e. the Malikis] more beloved to me than Shafi'i" (IAH 77). Even if this accolade is pure invention, Shafi'i's eventual burial in the 'Abd al-Hakam family plot attests to their continued ties.

SHAFI'I'S DEATH, FUNERAL, AND BURIAL

Shafi'i died at age fifty-four at the very end of Rajab 204 (January 820). Whatever physical weakness he manifested, his personality and intellect remained strong. A tale where Rabi', once again portrayed as a dim bulb, visits him shows Shafi'i in full command of his faculties. Rabi' relates: "I said to him, 'May God strengthen your weakness.' He said, 'If God strengthens my weakness, it will kill me.'" Another disciple narrates that Shafi'i taught him to say, instead, "May God strengthen your strength and weaken your weakness." Even *in extremis* Shafi'i kept his sense of humor and an acute awareness of the subtleties of language (IAH 274). Another account tells us that when Muzani visited him on his sickbed, Shafi'i recited poetry.

Shafi'i breathed his last at Ibn 'Abd al-Hakam's home in Fustat. Various accounts suggest that he died after the evening prayers, and thus (since the day begins at sunset) on Friday, the day of congregational prayers and an especially meritorious day for death. The 'Abd al-Hakam family extended its patronage to Shafi'i even after his death; his burial in the family plot attests to this, as does the designation of Ibn 'Abd al-Hakam as one of the executors of Shafi'i's will. (He had played this role for several others.)

SHAFI'I'S WILL

Shafi'i had drafted his will in Shaban 203/February 819. Preserved in the *Umm*, it gives us extremely valuable information about Shafi'i's connections, finances, and personal life. Inheritance law was developed enough by then that basic property division would be clear. Rules presented in the Qur'an had been elaborated by jurists including Shafi'i in mind-numbing detail. They provided for a fixed division of assets among classes of heirs. After appropriate pious formulae, the will addresses his provisions for those who do not automatically get a specified portion of his estate. Since wills do not address those who get fixed shares, his testament cannot tell us which of his relatives were living, except for his children who are mentioned in connection with their guardianship. A decedent could bequeath up to a third of his or her estate (to non-heirs). He did so.

His bequests make reference to numerous other relationships that can help us to situate him in his time and context.

He was enmeshed in a variety of friendship, ownership, clientage, and patronage relationships. Among the slaves and freedpeople the will mentions is Fawz, an "Andalusian slave-girl" who was wet nurse to his infant son Abu'l-Hasan, born in Egypt when Shafi'i was in his early fifties. The will outlines several scenarios for Fawz's manumission. Barring complications, she would be freed when Abu'l-Hasan was weaned at the customary age of twenty-four months. Should the child die before then, Fawz would be freed immediately. If he should reach two years old but, for health reasons, it should be deemed preferable to delay weaning, then her manumission would be postponed until he turned three – or died in the interim. It is impossible to know whether Abu'l-Hasan had a sickly constitution, prompting Shafi'i's repeated reference to his son's potential death, or whether this was merely the inevitable outcome of his lawyerly instinct to address every possible contingency at a time of high infant mortality rates. In fact, Abu'l-Hasan is sometimes said to have died as a young child, after his father. Another source, though, suggests he outlived his father by more than two decades, dying in his late twenties in 231/846.

The will singles out another slave: Abu'l-Hasan's mother. Dananir (the plural of dinar – colloquially, "Coinage," "Moolah") was Shafi'i's concubine. Sexual relationships between male owners and their unmarried female slaves were legal and common. If a slave bore her master a child, the child was free and legitimate and the slave would become free at her master's death. This manumission is automatic so the will does not mention it. Instead, it sets forth Shafi'i's provisions for Dananir, including some which are worded to provide for possible further offspring, indicating that he continued to have sex with her. If she became pregnant again, a slavegirl or eunuch was to be bought for her, up to 25 dinars, or she was to be given 20 dinars as a legacy. The will expresses the expectation that Dananir would, at least in the short term, retain physical custody (but not legal guardianship) of Abu'l-Hasan and take him back to

Mecca, perhaps accompanied by Fawz. Of the twenty-four shares into which Shafi'i divides his bequeathable assets, two were to provide an income stream for the support of Dananir; a third share would provide for Fawz, should she choose to accompany the pair to Mecca.

He directed other bequests to Meccan relatives, associates, and dependants. Four twenty-fourths were allocated to Shafi'i's poor relations, descended from his ancestor Shafi' ibn al-Sa'ib, "young and old, male and female." Another five shares were allocated to purchasing the freedom of worthy slaves. The largest single bequest, six twenty-fourths or one quarter of the total, was for Muhammad ibn al-Walid al-Azraqi, a prominent Meccan whose family spawned several noted historians of the city. One or two shares were variously devoted to alms to Meccan neighbors, small legacies for Meccan freed clients of his and his mother's and so forth.

As he sets his affairs in order, Shafi'i swings between Egyptian and Meccan concerns. He names two additional Egyptians as executors but the testament repeatedly refers to Mecca and to his close connections to that city. Several months prior, in a document also preserved, he had made alterations to the deed of two houses owned there, putting them into a charitable trust or endowment that allowed him to direct the proceeds to one heir over others – in this case, his infant son Abu'l-Hasan and Abu'l-Hasan's eventual descendants; should that line die out, to his daughters. (He made similar arrangements for a house in Egypt, according to an undated document.) One further issue related to his children: the will designates guardians for his offspring by his wife suggesting that they had yet to reach majority when he wrote it. Perhaps, then, Shafi'i was closer to forty than to thirty when he became a father.

What scant evidence exists of Shafi'i's personal relationships reveals someone utterly at ease with the social inequalities of his era. He accepted legal hierarchies of freedom, gender, ethnicity, and religion – ones that placed him as a free Arab Muslim male at the top of the heap. He insisted in his jurisprudence on the obligation of those at the top to take the best interests of those below into account, and seems to have tried to care for those he saw as his dependents and inferiors. As is to be expected, slavery gave him no moral qualms. In addition to his concubine, and his son's wet nurse, his biographers mention a Slavic youth, at least two eunuchs, and a slavegirl whom he bought to cook for him, assuring her that he would not approach her sexually. Another document makes reference to a brown eunuch named Salih, a Nubian breadmaker possibly named Bulbul, a slave from Fez named Salim, and a brown female slave the possession of whom he left in trust for his son. It is unclear if he owned all of these slaves simultaneously or whether they were divided between households in Mecca and Egypt. He manumitted some, and made provision for their support, but there is no sign that he had any intention of erasing distinctions of wealth or status.

His relationships with free women of his own social stratum are obscure. His mother was clearly an important force in his life, but we know little about her. We also know little about his relationships with his daughters. Like virtually every other jurist of his time, Shafi'i affirmed the father's privilege to marry off his minor daughters without their consent, and like Malik (but not the Iraqis) he extended this power to the first marriage of even post-pubescent daughters. At the same time, he strongly advocated consulting daughters as to their wishes – supporting his stance with relevant prophetic precedent – and presumably he did so with his own offspring. He was, Ibn Abi Hatim tells us, concerned about honor and zealously guarded his womenfolk's chastity: when one of the two young eunuchs he owned reached puberty, he ignored the fair amount of license typically allotted to castrated male servants and prevented him from having access to the women of his household, buying another in his place to serve the women.

Hierarchies of gender are intertwined with those of ethnicity. Shafi'i's protective instincts encompass Arab women generally; their status depends on avoiding disreputable alliances. I mentioned earlier Shafi'i's sense of ethnic superiority with regard to linguistic skill. More broadly, the general climate in Iraq and Egypt was one of both real and perceived threats to Arab supremacy. But Shafi'i's Arab pride carried over into matters of marriage. Rabi' reports, "I asked Shafi'i about a [non-Arab] client (*mawla*) marrying an Arab woman, and he said, 'I am an Arab. Don't say that to me.'" Rabi' notes, though, that he is making a point about social acceptability not law: "If it were forbidden, he would have said, 'It is not valid'" (IAH 293). Shafi'i objects to an Arab woman marrying below her station but little opprobrium attached to men marrying beneath themselves. Still, he married a woman of impressive Arab lineage and kept a concubine of inferior status and unknown ethnic origin.

The emotional tenor of Shafi'i's marriage remains inaccessible to us except in one or two glimpses. He and his wife may have loved and teased one another, for Ibn Khallikan reports that Shafi'i jested: "I had a wife and I loved her, and when I saw her, I said to her: 'It is an unfortunate thing to love one who loves you not.' She retorted, in the same poetic meter: 'She averts her face, and you entreat her, but succeed not'" (IAH 312, IK 2:572). Bayhaqi's voluminous biography includes a solitary domestic recollection, suggesting that though Shafi'i was perceived by his underlings as a fearsome figure, his wife was comfortable joking with him. His daughter Zaynab recalls that a wet nurse entered a room where her mother was awake and her father was sleeping. When the servant's young son began to cry, she was afraid that the noise would awaken the master. Dreading this, she firmly covered the child's mouth, nearly suffocating him in the attempt to leave the room quietly. When Shafi'i later awoke, his wife teased him about it, calling him Ibn Idris and saying he nearly plotted a slaughter. In one version of the tale, he blushed in response.

As for professional relationships with women, it was not unusual for male scholars to have female students and even to study with female teachers. No woman appears as one of his major disciples or transmitters, although Muzani's sister, the mother of the noted Hanafi scholar al-Tahawi, is sometimes said to have been his student. The only woman who could conceivably be counted among

Shafi'i's teachers is Sayyida Nafisa (d. 208/824), whose biographers report that Shafi'i heard hadith from her; his biographers mention nothing of the sort. There are accounts of him speaking to unrelated women, including the mother of Bishr al-Marisi (d. 218/833), a theologian who studied with both Sufyan ibn 'Uyayna and Abu Yusuf. This is not surprising if, as Bishr's biographical accounts assert, Shafi'i lived with him and his mother for a time in Baghdad.

Shafi'i knew of the personal lives of his associates, though he presumably did not socialize with the women of their households. When Rabi' married, Shafi'i asked how much he had given his wife as dower. On learning that Rabi' had fixed a thirty-dinar dower but only paid six, Shafi'i immediately provided Rabi' with the remaining twenty-four dinars. This anecdote gives us at one stroke Shafi'i's generosity, his concern for his student, and his preference for prompt payment of dower.

SHAFI'I'S FINANCIAL PERSONALITY

To a generation raised on the merits of saving for a rainy day, Shafi'i's reported dealings with money might seem odd, perhaps feckless. He was repeatedly in straits as an adult, going bankrupt three times in his life in one account. Persistently impecunious, it is said that he pledged his house as security against a loan in order to raise funds for his journey to Yemen and borrowed money from Ibn 'Abd al-Hakam to get established in Egypt. According to another source, Shafi'i was so broke that he sold what little he had, until his daughter and wife went hungry; despite his financial difficulties, this account says he never pledged anything (IAH 126). Yet his will shows him to be wealthy: the third of his estate he is permitted to bequeath was sufficient, at least as of the will's drafting, to be divided into twenty-four shares.

We can only guess at how he acquired money and supported his family. Various accounts show him receiving and spending staggering sums: the 50,000 dirhams from the caliph Harun al-Rashid, in one instance (which makes the fifty or sixty dinars he is said to have paid for copies of Shaybani's writings seem like small change), or arriving in Mecca from Sanaʻa with 10,000 dinars. Another source suggests that he was 70,000 dirhams (3500 dinars) in debt when he died.

For the period around Shafiʻi's life, M. M. Ahsan has extrapolated the cost of goods and services, speculatively, from various sources. One can very roughly estimate his main expenses for clothing, food, and shelter. In the year of his death, in Mosul an average-quality tunic (*qamis*) sold for around two dinars. (During Muhammad's era ten to twelve dirhams equaled one dinar, but exchange rates fluctuated.) Several decades earlier, in Basra, a wrap known as an *izar* sold for 6.5 dirhams; a century later, around twenty-two, and in Mosul, the range was between six and eighteen dirhams; as always, luxury goods were substantially more expensive. Women's clothing was similarly priced, and Shafiʻi would have been obliged to provide at least one outfit per season for his wife and daughters. Food prices during his adult lifetime were remarkably low in Iraq – dates were not always and everywhere as cheap as in Basra, where a tray could be had for a third of a dirham, but they were plentiful during stable times. Ascetics might subsist on meager rations and the courtly elite expend ridiculous sums, but a more ordinary expenditure for food might be around five dirhams per day per person, or between ten dirhams and 1 dinar daily for a middle-class family. Rented quarters might cost a bachelor around five dirhams per month – substantially less than food, certainly – and a modest house could cost anywhere from thirty dinars to 2000 dirhams. This puts Rabiʻ's wife's thirty dinar dower in perspective, but it also indicates that either Shafiʻi was reckless with large sums or the story is a significant embellishment, or perhaps both.

Shafiʻi, we are told, gave freely in charity. Having come into a windfall, he gave it away until nothing remained. Of course the caliphal largesse and bankruptcies need not be literally true. Even if they were, it is not necessarily the case that he was shockingly bad with money. Major reversals of fortune (financial as well as political) were common. And rather than viewing prudent accumulation of wealth against future needs as admirable, his biographers would have been inclined to laud his unwillingness to hoard. Stories about Muhammad's Companions outdoing one another in their charitable giving present an impractical set of guidelines for life but a clear moral vision. Thus, as Shafi'i's biographers wove stories about wealth and charity into the narrative of his life, they made sure to portray him as generous rather than miserly. But compared to biographers of figures who, like Ibn Hanbal, are recognized primarily for their pious virtues, they paid relatively little attention to ascetic scruples concerning the consumption of illicit wealth or avoiding beholdenness to rulers. It is, therefore, somewhat mysterious how Shafi'i came to be remembered and venerated for his saintly virtues in addition to his scholarly ones. I will return to his legacy after discussing his work.

LEGAL THEORY I
The Risala, *Sunna, and Hadith*

Shafi'i's study with Malik in Medina was formative, and his first Iraqi period transformative. His time in Mecca and, again, Iraq allowed his method and teachings to develop independently. It was in Egypt, however, that his thought bore its most important fruit. Shafi'i's half-dozen Egyptian years were extraordinarily productive. Some reports say he spent half his days writing. Others explain his prolific corpus by diligent work habits plus a divine nudge. Asked about how Shafi'i accomplished so much in his short time, Ibn Rahawayh replied that God consolidated his intelligence because of the shortness of his life. But no supernatural explanation is required. His accomplishments in Egypt were the culmination of decades of study and thought, emerging in his teaching, debating, and writing. Moreover, some of the books that were in a crucial sense products of his intellect nonetheless were not compiled during his lifetime.

SHAFI'I'S BOOKS

Muhammad al-Hasan ibn Muhammad al-Marwazi attributes 113 books of law, exegesis, *belles lettres* (*adab*), and various other topics to Shafi'i. Not all of these were major or polished works — some would have been short treatises or chapters in larger works, others notebooks used for teaching — and not all have survived. Of these, the *Risala* is best known. Hamid Algar has written that: "[T]he history of Islam as an intellectual and spiritual tradition consists above all of its scholars and the works that they wrote; the book is the quintessential artifact of Islamic civilization" (2002, 17). If one were to write a history of Islam as a series of great books, Shafi'i's *Risala* would figure prominently. His other writings on legal theory and method include the *Summation of Knowledge*, the *Invalidation of Juristic Preference*, *Disagreements between Hadith*, and short treatises such as *Disagreements between the Two Iraqis*. To an even greater extent than the *Risala*, these debate and dissect methodological differences, in tones sometimes even-tempered, sometimes rudely polemical. Shafi'i also authored – for a given value of that term – two major works of substantive law. The former, known as the *Hujja*, held his Meccan and Iraqi teaching – his "old" doctrine. The latter, which alone survives, is known as the *Umm*, but is routinely titled the *Mabsut* in earlier lists of his works.

This chapter discusses the *Risala* and its key ideas: prophetic sunna as revelation, hadith as the proper means of knowing the sunna, and how the legal sources interact. It also addresses the treatment of hadith in Shafi'i's other methodological writings. The next chapter focuses on how revelation is to be interpreted to yield law – the uses and limits of human reason and the need for specialist expertise. The following chapter explores how Shafi'i's substantive jurisprudence in the *Umm* relates to his methodological principles.

THE *RISALA* AS A TEXT

Before we can consider the *Risala*'s content, we must deal briefly with the linked questions of authorship and authenticity. Tradition reports that Shafi'i wrote the *Risala* (*Epistle*) at the request of the Basran hadith scholar 'Abd al-Rahman ibn Mahdi (d. 198/813). This tale is likely an attempt to explain its title: the text displays no epistolary features. But *risala* can also indicate an introduction or an innovative, essayistic format for the expression of novel ideas rather than the transmission of inherited knowledge.

It is generally agreed — though we have little evidence to prove or disprove it — that two versions of the *Risala* existed. The old version, now lost, was composed in Iraq or, in a minority view, in Mecca. Shafi'i is said to have substantially revised it in Egypt, as he did with many of his substantive doctrines. (For these, unlike for the two versions of the *Risala*, there is proof: some older doctrines survive in quotations in Muzani's *Digest*.)

The *Risala* — which Chaumont (2006) calls "a radical critique of judicial conformism" — is conventionally reputed to have been the first work of legal theory (*usul al-fiqh*, literally, "principles" or "roots" of jurisprudence). The claim has been contested by some Hanafis, intent on granting that honor to Abu Yusuf. But Ibn Khaldun affirms Shafi'i's primacy in his *Muqaddimah* (*Prolegomenon*) and al-Fakhr al-Razi gloats that Shafi'i first organized the sources of law into a system, comparing his status in the field to Aristotle's status in logic.

Among specialists in early Islamic legal history, however, intense debates have been taking place over Shafi'i's legacy. Wael Hallaq (1993, 1997) has argued that Shafi'i's work was ignored for a century and, in any case, bore little resemblance to later legal theory. Norman Calder (1993), working on the basis of evidence internal to the text, challenged the attribution of the *Risala* to either Shafi'i's era or an individual author. Both of their claims, however, must be qualified or rejected. It has become clear that the *Risala* circulated shortly after its composition, attracting opposition. Devin Stewart (2002) notes that several sections of the manual written by Dawud al-Zahiri's son, Muhammad ibn Dawud (d. 297/910), clearly respond to the *Risala*, contesting Shafi'i's views on consensus and *ijtihad*. Murteza Bedir (2002) demonstrates that an early Hanafi, 'Isa ibn Aban (d. 221/835–6), criticized Shafi'i's ideas about prophetic reports (and was in turn criticized by Ibn Surayj, who also debated Muhammad ibn Dawud). Not all attention was negative: El Shamsy (2009) has shown definitively that the *Risala* can be dated through quotations in various early third/ninth-century works to nearly Shafi'i's own lifetime. There is the evidence of the manuscript for the *Risala* itself. Although the earliest extant complete manuscript of the *Risala* postdates Shafi'i by 500 years, a seventy-eight-folio manuscript survives with a mark indicating that Shafi'i's disciple Rabi' taught the text in 265/878–9. Scholars debate this attribution. Ahmad Shakir, responsible for the standard edition of the text, believes that the bulk of the text was copied by the student who read it aloud to Rabi', and that the permission to transmit the text is in Rabi''s own hand; skeptics have proposed instead a mid-fourth/tenth-century date. It seems unlikely that anyone will have the chance to revisit the question: long preserved in Egypt's national library, the manuscript was discovered to be missing in 2002 and is rumored to be in the hands of a Saudi collector.

What about the suggestion, though, that Shafi'i did not author the *Risala*? There are two issues here: whether the *Risala* can be attributed to a single author and whether that author is Shafi'i. Tracing the *Risala* to an individual author rather than a collective editing process over years or decades is fairly easy on formal grounds. The text stands as an internally consistent, self-contained unit, with an integrated argument and terminology, though it does switch from exposition to dialogue partway through. Although editing clearly took place at some juncture it seems safe to attribute the *Risala* to a single author.

Was this author Shafi'i? Plenty of premodern Arabic texts are attributed to figures who turn out not to have written them. Notions of authorship differed dramatically from contemporary standards, which prize originality. One might attribute not only individual positions but even whole works to one's teacher not out of plagiaristic intent – plagiarism falsely claims rather than falsely denies authorship – but to make one's words authoritative by putting them in the mouth of a recognized authority. There are good reasons to suppose that this is not the case here, though. Quotations and citations of the *Risala* in contemporaneous and slightly later works assert Shafi'i's authorship, even while Shafi'i remained a controversial figure. His reputation would not have lent an immediate gloss of authority to a text. Additionally, key features of its vocabulary and style, especially the interlocutor's voice against which Shafi'i often presents his arguments, accord with his other works, including the *Summation of Knowledge*. Consistency across these works suggests a unity of thought, a similar set of mental structures and concerns.

Yet those scholars who have questioned the foundational place of the *Risala* for Islamic law are on to something. Mature Sunni legal theory espouses a four-fold source scheme of Qur'an, prophetic example, consensus, and analogy. Conventional wisdom has long held that Shafi'i proposed this four-source method in the *Risala* to resolve a standoff between the adherents of tradition (*ahl al-hadith*) and the partisans of opinion (*ahl al-ra'y*). However, newer scholarship shows that the *Risala*, read carefully, does not present such a scheme. Instead, Shafi'i's legal hermeneutics, as Joseph Lowry has shown, center on the *bayan*, or normative statement, that constitutes God's communication to humanity. Shafi'i's vision that all legal rules can be derived from revealed texts – which he defines as Qur'an and prophetic sunna – in a fixed number of ways is both innovative and quite distinct from what eventually becomes the core of the later theoretical tradition. The *Risala*, though influential, did not singlehandedly set the agenda for legal theory. What it did do is promote Shafi'i's distinctive ideas about the dual nature of revelation, the exclusive authoritativeness of prophetic sunna as recorded in hadith, and his ideas about the necessary if subordinate role of human reason in extrapolating from revealed texts.

KEY IDEAS IN THE *RISALA*

The *Risala*, which runs to 601 pages in the heavily annotated standard Arabic edition and nearly 300 pages in its lightly footnoted English translation, is divided into several sections. Much of it is framed as a dialogue with an interlocutor who challenges Shafi'i repeatedly, allowing him to defend his views about revelation and its interpretation. Its interlocking topics include: the Qur'an, prophetic example (which he defines as a kind of revelation), hadith (the vehicle for transmitting prophetic example and thereby revelation), analysis of language (to interpret revelation), issues of contradiction and non-contradiction (to apply revelation), and abrogation (as a sub-topic regarding contradiction in revelation, or rather how to avoid it). Consensus is dealt with more or less summarily near the end of the work. Independent reasoning (*ijtihad*) receives more attention, as it is more closely linked to the key concern of the *Risala*: how to delimit and interpret divine communication to humanity.

The *Risala* draws on broader currents of second/third- and eighth/ninth-century views about revelation and language. These were the province not only of legal thinkers but also of theologians and grammarians. Shafi'i borrows debate techniques from the former and technical terminology from the latter. He molds them into a theory of the law, whereby God's direct communication to humanity takes two forms: the Qur'an and Muhammad's example. These are both all-inclusive and utterly consistent: perceived lacunae or contradictions can be resolved by expert interpretation.

The *Risala* is best understood in concert with some of Shafi'i's other writings about legal method, especially two books on different aspects of hadith. These are the monograph *Ikhtilaf al-Hadith* (*Disagreements between Hadith*), and the short treatise *Jima' al-'Ilm* (*Summation of Knowledge*). They present variations on some of the *Risala*'s arguments. *Disagreements between Hadith* focuses on how one reconciles seemingly contradictory traditions about the words and actions of Islam's Prophet. The *Summation* is an extended argument for the need to accept hadith as a source of law, although it also touches on the question of independent legal interpretation and consensus.

As with many positions superseded by subsequent orthodoxies, we know of alternate views in part due to criticisms of them in the works of the victors. What we know about opposition to the use of sunna as a major source of law, and to hadith as the main repository of sunna, comes from depictions of the losers' views in the writings of the winners. The *Summation* is aimed squarely at those who reject hadith. Although one can be certain that the views of his opponents are not portrayed in their most flattering light, the types of objections to Shafi'i's doctrine raised by his debate partner(s) seem plausible. Some objected to using any hadith as a source of law, and others objected to a subset of hadith which they deemed unreliable. Shafi'i tackles both sets of objections by insisting that obedience to God is necessary, something none dispute; that following prophetic sunna is absolutely necessary for obedience to God, something some dispute; and that this sunna is reliably preserved in hadith form. This last point is the crucial stumbling block and thus one of the main targets of his arguments. The *Summation* also argues that sunna does not contradict itself or the Qur'an but merely requires expert handling to yield legal determinations. Muslims need these determinations to obey God.

How do these three works fit into the chronology of Shafi'i's life? The *Summation* probably predates the *Risala*. As Aisha Musa notes, portions of the *Risala* lack "the relentless, confrontational tone" of their counterparts in the *Summation*, suggesting a more mature presentation of ideas (2008, 59). El Shamsy observes, moreover, that the second section of the *Summation* speaks specifically to the arguments around hadith made by the Iraqi Ibrahim ibn 'Ulayya (d. 218/833), and that it may have been composed in Baghdad when Shafi'i debated with him (though they are also said to have debated in Egypt). Further, the *Risala* incorporates the arguments about revelation from the *Summation* and the concerns about interpretation addressed in *Disagreements between Hadith* into a coherent totality: it represents a cogent final statement of Shafi'i's doctrine. Nonetheless, the key ideas expressed in the three texts largely coincide, and hence I will address them together.

PROPHETIC EXAMPLE

The most important contribution Shafi'i made to Muslim civilization was his conviction that prophetic hadith was a necessary and unique supplement to the Qur'an as a source of law. Of course, he was not the first to value prophetic precedent or reports. Muhammad was universally respected and revered among Muslims, as prophet, community leader, and moral exemplar. His wife Aisha declared "His character is the Qur'an" and Qur'an 33:21 refers to him as "a good model" or "a beautiful example." During his lifetime, he was consulted on everything from ritual practice to familial disputes to date cultivation. (In response to the news that his advice had resulted in a poor harvest, he responded that in agricultural matters, his advice was no better than that of any other person, and in fact much less to be trusted than that of someone with expertise: next time, ask a date farmer instead.) After his death, his Companions remembered his actions and decisions. Yet, despite their overwhelming reverence for the Prophet, they did not justify all their subsequent deeds by explicit reference to his practice or sunna. The caliphs who succeeded him made decisions on their own authority. Moreover, the caliphs themselves, especially Abu Bakr and 'Umar, were also considered authoritative models. The emerging class of jurists referred back to the Companions' words and deeds as well as Muhammad's in justifying their decisions.

Shafi'i fundamentally reshaped the way sunna was understood, considerably narrowing its scope. First, he defined sunna as exclusively prophetic. Second, he insisted that properly transmitted hadith were the sole means of knowing the sunna. Third, he argued that sunna was co-equal to the Qur'an as a source of law and, in fact, was a form of revelation. William Graham has argued that the early Muslim community's understanding of Muhammad's prophethood included both "verbatim Qur'anic revelation" and "implicit, non-Qur'anic revelation granted him as a function of his prophethood" as essential parts of "God's revelatory activity" (1977, 19). To see the activity of Shafi'i and those who came after him as an epistemological break overlooks or misrepresents an essential element of community understanding. Nonetheless, it is certainly the case that among legal scholars, Shafi'i proposed something novel by defining sunna in the way he did.

In addition to restricting sunna to that of Muhammad, he argued strenuously that the only acceptable repository for such sunna was transmitted reports. Medinans upheld the practice of their community not as a departure from or counterweight to prophetic precedent but as its most authentic embodiment. Others, including Iraqis like Abu Hanifa, assumed that Companions' practices would naturally reflect prophetic precedent, and thus that accounts of their words and deeds were legally authoritative. Shafi'i dissented on both counts. He not only insisted on solely prophetic precedent but also that hadith reports with chains of reliable transmitters were the appropriate means of verification of this prophetic information. Reliable transmitters provide a reasonable certainty with regard to prophetic tradition; one can thus rely on it to guide practice. In the absence of such authentic hadith, he allowed a Companion's precedent to carry authority. However, even a tradition from the Prophet reported by a lone individual without corroboration trumps any other non-Qur'anic proof.

HADITH IN SHAFI'I'S THOUGHT

Shafi'i's defense of prophetic sunna in the form of properly authenticated hadith is central to the *Risala* and even more prominent in his *Summation of Knowledge*. It plays a role in his substantive jurisprudence as well, despite the fact that Shafi'i was a lackluster traditionist. Bukhari's terse entry for him in the *Kitab al-Tarikh al-Kabir* follows his name with four spare bits of data: "Muhammad ibn Idris, Abu 'Abdallah al-Shafi'i al-Qurashi: Lived in Egypt, died in the year 204, heard [hadith from] (*sami'a*) Malik ibn Anas, Hijazi." The entry, as the case for the vast majority of other entries, mostly serves to identify him by his name and does not formally assess his reliability as a transmitter.

Nonetheless, as proficiency with hadith increasingly became a gauge of one's scholarly and even moral credentials in certain Sunni circles, Shafi'i's biographers felt compelled to defend his prowess as a hadith critic and transmitter. Bayhaqi devotes several sections of his *Shafi'i's Virtues* (1971) to enumeration of instances where Shafi'i recognized defects in the transmission of hadith. Abu al-'Abbas al-Asamm (d. 346/957), one of Rabi''s students, compiled a *Musnad* containing all of the traditions cited by Shafi'i in the *Umm* and the *Risala*. The later Shafi'i scholar Shahrazuri reports a dream visit where the Prophet Muhammad, asked about this *Musnad*, replies "I said it, word for word." Asked about the more highly regarded collections of Bukhari and Muslim, as well as Malik's *Muwatta'*, the Prophet said merely that they were "sound" (Ibn Qadi Shubha 2003, 90). In another dreamer's vision, the Prophet disclaims support for Abu Hanifa and Malik's views, but calls Shafi'i's position "the opposite of the position of the innovators (*ahl al-bid'a*)" (IAH 73).

We may confidently set aside these exaggerated reports of hadith prowess without discounting Shafi'i's contribution to traditionalism, which lay not in his personal activity as a transmitter but as an advocate of prophetic hadith as a source of law. For this, he gained the title Defender of the Sunna. He responds incredulously when one hapless observer asks, after Shafi'i has recited a prophetic tradition, whether he follows it. The questioner uses the same language that is used to ask if one follows the doctrine of a particular scholar. Aghast at the possibility that one could know Muhammad's precedent on a matter and not consider it binding, Shafi'i replies: "When I know a tradition from the Messenger of God and I don't follow it, I bear witness to you, I will have lost my mind" (IAH 67).

SUNNA AS REVELATION

Shafi'i was far from the first to uphold the importance of prophetic hadith, but he broke with his contemporaries in considering it a second form of revelation of equal weight with the Qur'an and its sole acceptable supplement as a source of law. The *Risala* distinguishes between Qur'an and sunna only as a matter of use, not authoritativeness: the Qur'an is "recited" revelation – that is, recited in ritual prayer – and sunna is revelation that one does not recite. (Elsewhere, Shafi'i occasionally seems to waffle about whether one can call the Prophet's words revelation, but the *Risala* is clear on this point.)

Because he is proposing something novel, he must justify treating Qur'an and sunna as co-equal revelation. Like any good lawyer, he builds his case as a series of propositions, assent to one of which leads inexorably to the next. The fixed, authoritative Qur'anic text serves as a springboard. The Qur'an itself commands obedience to Muhammad, from which it follows that obedience to Muhammad requires accepting his sunna as revelation; moreover, knowledge of the sunna requires accepting hadith reports. These assertions require slightly fuller explanation.

Shafi'i's first argument, that the Qur'an commands obedience to Muhammad, is not itself controversial. He enters new territory where he identifies obedience to Muhammad with following the sunna. He quotes various Qur'anic verses, including 59:7, to drive home the point that "God has imposed the duty on men to obey his divine communications as well as the sunna of His Messenger" (*Risala* 110).

He takes another step when he argues that the sunna is a second form of revelation, interpreting Qur'anic references to "the Book and the Wisdom" as Qur'an and sunna. The *Risala* quotes Q. 2:146 ("And also we have sent among you a Messenger from among yourselves to recite to you our signs, and purify you, to teach you the Book and the Wisdom, and to teach you what you did not know"; *Risala* 110) and, in a similar vein, Q. 62:2, which also discusses the Messenger's duty to teach both God's Book and the Wisdom to an unlettered (or Gentile) community. In an unusual though not entirely unprecedented move, he identifies this Wisdom (*hikma*) as prophetic practice:

> I have heard that those who are learned in the Qur'an – whom I approve – hold that the Wisdom is the sunna of the Messenger of God. ... For the Qur'an is mentioned first, followed by Wisdom; [then] God mentioned His favor to humankind by teaching the Qur'an and Wisdom. So it is not permissible for Wisdom to be called here [anything] save the sunna of the Messenger of God. For [Wisdom] is closely linked to the Book of God and God has imposed the duty of obedience to his Messenger and imposed on men the obligation to obey his orders.
>
> (*Risala* 111–12)

In the *Summation*, Shafi'i's interlocutor asks whether the Book and the Wisdom might not be two terms for one thing. Shafi'i rejects this, calling on another verse (Q. 33:34) which says that "God's revelations and Wisdom" are being recited in the homes of the Prophet's wives. He says that these are distinct: the Prophet both recites Qur'an and explains it, as well as making other pronouncements.

Not everyone has this type of direct access to God's Messenger. Yet the obligation to obey God's Messenger falls equally "on everyone who actually saw His Messenger and on those thereafter until the Day of Judgment." Hadith reports are therefore necessary: "Anyone who is remote [in time] from beholding God's Messenger cannot know the commandment of God's Messenger except by means of a report from him" (Lowry, forthcoming). These hadith reports interact in a variety of ways with God's direct guidance in the Qur'an.

THE MODES OF THE *BAYAN*

Having established that there are two types of revelation, Shafi'i must then address the question of how they interact. Here the concerns of the *Summation* intersect with a major preoccupation of the *Risala*. Lowry has suggested that "what underlies the *Risala* as a whole is Shafi'i's attempt to account for all the possible ways in which the Qur'an and the Sunna express rules of law" (Lowry 2007, 61). There are five types of *bayan*, communications or normative statements that God makes to humanity. In the first type, the Qur'an conveys the information by itself. (The *Risala* defines this as "what the book has laid down with such clarity that nothing further" is required; *Risala* 76.) The Qur'an and sunna convey information jointly in both the second and third type. In the second, the Qur'anic rule "is self-sufficient and the sunna provides detail that is not strictly necessary for compliance with the law" (Lowry 2008, 507). In the third type, about which Shafi'i has a great deal to say, sunna provides a necessary elaboration or clarification of Qur'anic commands, details without which believers could not perform required duties. In the fourth type of *bayan*, the sunna legislates independently. (Other scholars have seen the *Risala* as focused on these three ways in which sunna serves as a source for law.) In the fifth and final type, God's commands are known "by means of inference and legal interpretation, based on the Qur'an and the Sunna" (Lowry 2008, 508).

These five types of communication receive uneven treatment in the *Risala*. Shafi'i considers the first largely self-evident; no one disputes that the Qur'an legislates or that such legislation is binding on believers. He does address, on occasion, how its parts relate to one another, and I will have more to say about that later. But he cares less about potential intra-Qur'anic conflict than about how sunna functions as a source of law.

Though some obligations are sufficiently explained in the Qur'an, many are not. The *Risala* points out that the Qur'an commands prayer, almsgiving, and pilgrimage but omits detailed instructions about how to perform them. (The *Summation* uses prayer, almsgiving, and inheritance to make the same point.) Since God would not leave Muslims without guidance, God has supplemented the Qur'an with Muhammad's sunna. The Qur'anic command to obey Muhammad ("take what he gives you and leave what he forbids you"; Q. 59:7) means that his precedent should be followed where the Qur'anic text is silent. Take the case of prayer.

Several verses impose prayer on believers but the Qur'an provides few specifics. How many daily prayers? When? Using what liturgical language and formulae? What postures? Despite scriptural silence, all Muslims know how to pray. Muhammad's practice provided the details of these obligations: five daily prayers at dawn, midday, afternoon, sunset, and night; each cycle to include standing recitation, bowing, prostration, and certain utterances. By example, he showed which prayers were to be prayed silently and which aloud. He demonstrated through his words and deeds how one ought to pray behind a prayer leader.

Using reports from Muhammad to supplement Qur'anic guidance when the Book is insufficient and the hadith broadly agree with each other is not controversial. Shafi'i says in the *Risala* that scholars do not disagree about the acceptability of the sunna supplementing the Qur'an, although it seems that he was the first to formulate a theoretical justification for common practice. But he acknowledges dispute about the legitimacy of the fourth type of *bayan*, "what the Messenger has established as sunna and concerning which there is no text in the Book" (*Risala* 120, modified). Can sunna legislate independently? Here is where he turns to the notion of obedience, insisting that obedience to the Messenger is commanded in the Qur'anic text, and thus "the sunna for which there is no text in the Book" (*Risala* 122) is entirely binding: "the obligation to accept [these sunnas] rests upon us by virtue of the duty imposed by God to obey [the Prophet's] orders" (*Risala* 180).

In treating the question of sunna's independent legislative authority, Shafi'i's interlocutor raises the question of potential contradictions between sunna and Qur'an. Shafi'i denies that there could be any such conflict: "It is evident that the sunna never contradicts the Book of God, and that his sunna is binding even in the absence of legislation in the Book ... in accordance with God's command to obey his Messenger" (*Risala* 167, modified). But he cannot merely dismiss the topic, since apparent conflict between sunna and Qur'an, or between hadith, calls into question the usefulness and validity of hadith as an authoritative source.

Shafi'i insists stubbornly that there are no contradictions within the Qur'an, between authentic hadith and the Qur'an, or among authentic hadith. Those with sufficient knowledge and skill – specialists, like himself – can resolve these issues. He mounts an array of interpretive techniques, such as the classification of legal language, largely to avoid contradictions within and between scriptural texts. Any apparent conflicts are simply the result of texts applying to different cases, modifying each other in ways that relate to the circumstances of their revelation, or even abrogating one another. He draws on an arsenal of interpretive pairs, of which the two most important are *jumla/nass* (undefined versus "hermeneutically self-sufficient"; Lowry 2004, 37) and *'amm/khass* (general versus particular). He also relies on the concept of abrogation, the cancellation of one scriptural text by a later one. But before calling these techniques into play, he also explores in more depth a major objection raised by opponents of using prophetic sunna as a source of law: that of the reliability of the texts that record it.

SOURCE RELIABILITY

Those who oppose the use of hadith as a legal source focus on its reliability. Thus, Shafi'i devotes considerable attention to how one detects defective hadith. Most issues concern the reliability of transmitters. Shafi'i's interlocutors are concerned that hadith are epistemologically less certain than the Qur'an; therefore, some hold, they should not be used. Shafi'i objects. In the *Risala*, the *Summation*, and *Disagreements between Hadith*, he asserts that hadith are superior to witness testimony, which all accept as a basis for adjudication in certain matters. This is true even though a witness could be mistaken or lying. Even in capital crimes one must rely on witnesses; one can take life based on testimony. So if one employs more stringent standards for accepting a hadith transmission than for eyewitness reports – standards that rely not only on personal uprightness but also facts such as memory and clear understanding

— then accepting hadith as proof of the Prophet's words and deeds is even better justified.

Of course, not all hadith are reliable. One strategy that Shafi'i accepts, but where possible avoids, is to reject a defective tradition. Although one can reject a defective tradition to remove a perceived conflict between it and a Qur'anic text, the concept of defective traditions is of most use when attempting to reconcile traditions that conflict with one another. Shafi'i devotes a portion of the *Risala* to laying out things that make hadith texts unreliable. For the most part, he focuses here on unreliable transmission. In cases of seeming contradiction between hadith, one cause might be the unreliability of one of the texts. If so, one can discard it:

> one does not accept a hadith unless it is well established, just as he does not accept among witnesses any but those whose probity is known. So if the hadith [in question] is unknown or transmitted by an undesirable person, it is just as if it had not been transmitted at all, because it is not firmly established.
>
> (*Disagreements between Hadith*)

But one has the sense that he makes this point as a sop to his opponents: though he certainly acknowledges that not all hadith are reliable, he is far more interested in showing how perceived conflicts are only apparent rather than in throwing out suspect texts. In any case, this mechanism does not apply to the Qur'anic text; apparent conflicts within the Qur'an or between Qur'an and an authentic sunna, or between two authentic sunnas must be resolved using other strategies.

CONFLICTS BETWEEN TEXTS

Shafi'i repeatedly turns to the case of illicit sex, addressed in several Qur'anic verses and various hadith, to illustrate his other hermeneutical techniques for reconciling disparate pronouncements. Illicit sex is a notoriously complicated subject. Q. 4:19–20 mandates that four witnesses testify against women who commit "indecency" and that such women be detained in their houses "until death takes them or God appoints for them a way" (*Risala* 187, 230). Q. 24:2 prescribes a penalty of 100 lashes for any male or female who has illicit intercourse (*zina'*). In order to reconcile these two rules, Shafi'i utilizes abrogation (*naskh*). Abrogation means roughly that a later revelation cancels the ruling in an earlier revelation. In this case, "detainment as a punishment ... has been abrogated" by the later revelation commanding lashes.

The matter is not so simple, however. The lashing verse must be harmonized with other Qur'anic and prophetic texts. These include Q. 4:25, which states that female slaves who commit lewdness are liable to half the punishment of free women, and various prophetic hadith that impose stoning on those who engage in illicit sex. He uses these texts to further particularize the flogging verse, appealing to a distinction between general and particular or restricted and unrestricted provisions. The verse discussing half-punishment for female slaves, he says, shows that stoning applies only to free people. (Note that he makes an interpretive decision here to include male slaves along with female slaves as recipients of a half-penalty, even though they are not explicitly mentioned in the exception-text, and to take the verse's term "*muhsinat*" – that is, protected or chaste women – to apply to free women generally, not *married* free women specifically, as we will see in a moment.)

Here, one Qur'anic verse restricts the application of another. A sunna rule shows the Qur'anic penalty to have further restricted applicability. In both the *Risala* and the *Summation*, Shafi'i notes that the Prophet ordered some guilty parties to be stoned rather than lashed. He reconciles these rules by noting that stoning pertains to married (and, as Q. 4:25 shows, free) individuals, and lashing to never-married (or enslaved) individuals. Thus, he avoids contradiction.

In the *Summation*, Shafi'i appeals to this disjunction in order to convince his interlocutor of the need to accept sunna as a source of rules. Again, we see evidence of a divergent position through its citation by an opponent, as Shafiʻi notes that some people, presumably a marginal group, held that stoning ought not to be applied to anyone as a punishment for illicit sex because it would contravene the Qur'anically mandated lashes. His interlocutor agrees with him that stoning is the appropriate penalty but then must concede that hadith reports can modify Qur'anic legislation: otherwise there is no authoritative basis for stoning.

Shafiʻi grants sunna authority to elaborate on or demonstrate the restricted applicability of Qur'anic legislation. However, he rejects the notion that one type of revelation could abrogate the other. In contrast to the majority of those thinkers who accepted abrogation (not everyone did), and indeed to later members of his school who found Shafiʻi's position insufficiently robust to address all cases, Shafiʻi held that only a Qur'anic verse could abrogate a Qur'anic verse, and that only a new sunna could abrogate an old one. Where there seems to be contradiction, most often the sunna shows that a Qur'anic command that seems to be general has restricted applicability.

It is on Qur'anic edicts and sunna precedents for punishments for illicit sex and theft and specific details of performing pre-prayer ablution that the *Summation* concludes. Its final words affirm that "There will never be a Sunna that contradicts the Qur'an. God Most High is the Grantor of Success" (*Summation*, 155).

TECHNICAL VOCABULARY, LINGUISTIC AMBIGUITY, AND ARABIC

Near the beginning of the *Summation*, Shafiʻi relates a gripe conveyed by a hadith-rejecter which seems, at first blush, to be unrelated to the problem of hadith. Given that God calls the Qur'an "an explanation of all things," this interlocutor challenges:

> How can you allow yourself, or anyone else, to say of something that God has made obligatory that in one case the obligation is general; however, in another case it is specific; and in one case the command is

obligatory; however, in another case the command is a suggestion, and if he wishes, it is an expression of permissibility?

(*Summation* 115)

He then goes on to suggest that Shafi'i bases such seemingly whimsical views on hadith which are susceptible to error. Shafi'i's response focuses on the need to accept hadith, as discussed above. But what I wish to focus on here is the possibility of interpretive multiplicity within authentic texts, something that connects to Shafi'i's larger ideas about language and interpretation.

One difficulty for Shafi'i – related to his concern with contradiction – is when two authentic texts seem to apply divergent rules to the same situation. In this case, one must weigh their respective levels of obligation. This raises a larger question about imperative language, both positive and negative – that is, commands and prohibitions. Commands convey varying degrees of obligation, from absolute requirement to recommendation to mere permission (as the example of ablution will show). Prohibitions, likewise: something can be entirely forbidden, strongly warned against, or simply discouraged. There is a difference, of course, between what can be juridically enforced and what is ethically desirable. Jurisprudence deals with these matters routinely – to paraphrase one scholar, Islamic law is Islamic ethics – and Shafi'i notes that a legally valid action is not always a desirable one.

Shafi'i's argument in the *Risala* proceeds through a combination of dialogue with an imaginary interlocutor and detailed exposition of example problems, of which there are about sixty. Each addresses particular methodological points, sometimes explicitly and sometimes implicitly. Despite the atomistic example problems, key themes – the importance of sunna, the coherence of revelation, the need for expert interpretation – surface continually. For instance, Shafi'i's concern with avoiding contradiction suffuses the *Risala* even where the putative focus is on the need for the sunna to flesh out duties for which Qur'anic guidance is insufficient. This is Shafi'i's overt point in a discussion of ablution: "The Messenger laid down sunnas regulating ablution ... for such matters have not been dealt with in the Book" (*Risala* 153). The Qur'an commands: "wash your faces and your hands up to the elbows and wipe your heads and your feet up to the ankles" before prayer (Q. 5:6). But believers need further information to carry out this purification effectively. Fortunately, prophetic sunna elaborates. "Shafi'i said: The Messenger laid down sunna for ablution in conformity with God's communication." Shafi'i presents two separate hadith with full chains of transmitters recounting how Muhammad performed ablution. In the first, we learn that he washed "each limb once." In the second, the narrator calls for water and provides a full demonstration, which includes washing his face three times rather than once.

Shafi'i shows here how sunna provides information needed to complete a duty mandated but only vaguely described in the Qur'an. Yet his two proof texts diverge on the number of required washings, raising the specter of contradiction. Neither hadith can be dismissed as inauthentic. Neither abrogates the other. Neither applies to a different class of individuals. Shafi'i settles on the explanation that involves varying levels of command. Since the Prophet prayed after washing only once, this must be an adequate performance of the duty. Given that the sources suggest that he "ordinarily performed the ablution three times," Shafi'i decides that the three washings "were intended to be optional, not obligatory, so that the performance of less than that number would not be regarded as failure to fulfill the duty." Muhammad's sunna is not carelessly confusing but deliberately varied. Expert interpretation can discern not only the range of acceptable ways in which to perform ablution but also the varying levels of obligation attached to each.

ARABIC LANGUAGE

This ablution example also highlights Shafi'i's concern for the nuances of Arabic language. It is not just circumstances and situations that lead to potential contradiction. Sometimes it is a question of language itself. The command "wash" is ambiguous in its scope (what is to be washed?), in its method (how is the washing to be carried out?), and its level of obligations (is washing required or recommended?). Issues of apparent meaning and possible additional meanings are a crucial part of the interpretive enterprise. This ambiguity ensures a role for interpreters steeped in Arabic since, as he puts it in the *Summation*, "The language of the Arabs is vast" (*Summation* 119).

David Vishanoff suggests that Shafi'i hinges his legal theory on the concept of linguistic ambiguity. By "exploit[ing] linguistic ambiguity" within revealed texts, jurists can justify existing legal doctrines by interpreting revealed sources. Shafi'i is deeply interested in words and language. Adapting grammatical terms into legal usage allows him to approach revealed texts with powerful interpretive techniques. Of particular import is his classification of legal speech into "apparent" (*zahir*), "ambiguous" (*mujmal*), and "unambiguous" (*nass*). He also coins or modifies several legal terms, including general or unrestricted (*'amm*) and particular or restricted (*khass*), giving them technical meanings that allow them to serve their purpose of interpreting divine communication (the *bayan*). This focus on the language of texts and, in particular, "the discourse about degrees of clarity and ambiguity helps law-oriented theorists to achieve maximum default legal meaning and maximum interpretive flexibility simultaneously." In other words, jurists could interpret texts many ways, depending on how they chose to treat their language; at the same time, they could claim that their interpretations were "the plain and obvious meaning of the revealed texts" (Vishanoff 2011, 5, 2).

Attending carefully to the minute inflections, vocabulary, and echoes of Arabic, Shafi'i insists on the centrality of linguistic expertise for interpretation. The Qur'an is an exclusively Arabic book, in his view, and Arabic an undeniably superior language. It is less clear whether he thinks Arabs superior to non-Arabs. Lowry believes that "Shafi'i offers a theory of divinely sanctioned ethno-linguistic superiority" when he asserts that "The people most entitled to superiority in regard to language are those whose language is the language of the Prophet" (2007, 295–6). El Shamsy demurs: it is linguistic mastery that is essential, not ethnicity. Certainly part of Arabic's superiority, as the language of revelation, is that it is capable of nearly infinite gradations of meaning. Though perhaps in exceptional cases non-Arabs might attain the requisite skill to interpret revelation, I tend to agree with Lowry that Shafi'i believed Arabs were inherently better qualified. Shafi'i's admirers, of course, praise his superior command of the Arabic language – Jahiz (d. 255/868), himself a master manipulator of language, compared Shafi'i's utterances to "strung pearls," while referring to him as "the Mutallibi," calling his prestigious Arabic heritage to mind (B 260–1).

4

LEGAL THEORY II
Analogy, Ijtihad, *and Consensus*

The long-standing view of Shafi'i's major accomplishment in the *Risala* has been this: with the notion of *qiyas*, or a restricted analogical reasoning based on explicit revealed texts, Shafi'i brokered a compromise between the partisans of opinion, on the one hand, and the advocates of tradition on the other. With one master stroke, he curtailed the freewheeling rationalists and expanded the scope of matters that traditionalists could consider. It is this use of *qiyas* that leads some, like Abu Zahra (1948, 25), to make the claim that Shafi'i invented a new jurisprudence, "not the jurisprudence of the people of Medina alone, or the jurisprudence of the people of Iraq alone, but rather a marriage between them." There is certainly merit to the view of Shafi'i taking what he had learned from both the Medinans and the Iraqis, but his vision of a human reason wedded to scripture is best understood within his larger scheme of God's communication to humanity. In the fifth type of *bayan*, in the absence of a text from Qur'an or sunna a believer is commanded to use indicators in the texts and in the world to arrive at a ruling. This is not only a statement about how revelation works but also about how human servanthood works: God creates and commands and people are obligated to obey.

QIYAS AND IJTIHAD

Revelation, for Shafi'i, provides guidance for all situations. However, believers sometimes face situations for which revealed texts fail to yield immediately obvious guidance. The texts contain rules for people to follow in all circumstances, but human interpretive effort is sometimes necessary to discern them. His goal is to define how human interpretive effort may legitimately fill in the gaps left (deliberately, as we will see later) in revelation. Human reason cannot operate alone and relying simply on unfettered opinion could be disastrous. Views differ and change and, moreover, there is no warrant for this in the sources. To rely on unrestricted operations of human reason is to deny the comprehensiveness of God's communication to humanity. It is through the mechanism of *qiyas* or *ijtihad* that "a finite body of revealed texts may be rendered relevant to the infinite complexity of human events" (Calder 1983, 61). Neither *ijtihad*, independent legal interpretation, nor *qiyas* (roughly, analogical reasoning), which Shafi'i treats as largely interchangeable, is a source of law. Rather, they are tools, which he explains how to use.

In both the *Risala* and the *Summation*, Shafi'i uses the example of finding the direction of prayer when one is not within sight of the Ka'ba to illustrate how independent legal interpretation works. The Qur'an commands believers to turn toward the "sacred mosque" when it is prayer time. However, if one cannot see the Ka'ba, one must rely on other indicators of its direction, including signs, such as stars, in the natural world created by God. One does the best one can. It is not in actually getting the direction correct that one fulfills God's command, but rather in attempting to do so. Similarly, all agree that judges and muftis have used *ijtihad* "in matters for which there was no proof text from the Book of God, nor a Sunna of His Messenger" (*Summation* 127). Their behavior is evidence for the permissibility of using *ijtihad* – and, because Shafi'i's interlocutor demands a proof from sunna, Shafi'i cites (twice in the *Summation*) a hadith where the Prophet says that a judge who uses *ijtihad* is rewarded singly for being mistaken and doubly for being correct.

This sunna raises the possibility of error: even scholars will sometimes be wrong. They will not, however, be negligent; they are only commanded to obey to the best of their ability, just like the believer who is not responsible for actually facing the Ka'ba directly, only for attempting to do so. In addition to error, there will also be disagreement. People operating with the same indicators or texts may arrive at different conclusions on the basis of legitimate processes. It is not permissible in such a case for one to follow the other; rather, each should follow his own conclusion. This disagreement, which is both permissible and inevitable, is to be distinguished from unacceptable disagreement "about something for which there is a ruling proof text from God, or a Sunna from His Messenger ... or, a consensus of the Muslims" (*Summation* 146). It is only when no such text exists that independent reasoning is permissible; if he "then engages in *ijtihad* and his *ijtihad* differs from the *ijtihad* of someone else, it is permissible for him to hold one opinion and for someone else to hold another" (*Summation* 146).

Even as he recognizes the necessity of human reason in law, Shafi'i defines fairly narrowly the ways in which it can be used. *Ijtihad* is the term he usually uses when laypeople or scholars confront situations where they do not have all of the information that they need to make a decision. Sometimes it is merely a matter of informed guesswork using indicators, as in the case of locating the Ka'ba. Sometimes it is a case of seeing how things resemble one another. But at other times, a more specific analogy must guide the process of arriving at a decision. He refutes a view that one who breaks his Ramadan fast during the daytime by eating must fast twelve days to compensate, since God required fasting one month out of twelve. This, Shafi'i thinks, is nonsensical. One must have legal grounds for an analogy, not a mere proportional similarity. Shafi'i offers a rejoinder: "Say to him, God, Exalted and Majestic said: 'The night of destiny is better than a thousand months' [Qur'an 97:3], so the one who fails to pray on the night of destiny is obligated to pray for one thousand months, if one analogizes from his position" (IAH 285).

CONSENSUS

Another of the four sources of law that Shafi'i is typically, though inaccurately, credited with formulating into a system is consensus (*ijma'*), about which there comes to be significant disagreement. Is it the agreement of the entire Muslim populace? The agreement of the scholars? All scholars of a particular time? A specific place? Shafi'i says relatively little about it in the *Risala* and not much more elsewhere, and because he uses the term in at least three different senses over a number of years it is hard to pin down precisely what he means by it. It is clear that for him consensus is never a *source* of law; only the Qur'an and sunna are sources of law. In the *Risala*, it does have a place in the working of the law, though it dances at the edge of his *bayan* scheme. Shafi'i is generally an elitist about consensus, mostly using the term to refer to "the agreement of scholars and specialists, never to the agreement of Muslims at large" (Lowry 2007, 357).

Yet elsewhere Shafi'i refers to consensus as essentially universal agreement of the entire community. It may serve as an indicator when confronting an ambiguous Qur'anic text: "Its communications should be interpreted by the sunna of the Prophet; if no sunna is found, then by the consensus of the Muslims; if no consensus is possible, then by *qiyas*" (*Risala* 306). Here, consensus serves not as a legal source in and of itself but an after the fact proof that there had once been such a source, now inaccessible. The community as a whole "cannot be ignorant" of something established as sunna, nor agree that something is a sunna which is not (*Risala* 286). Here consensus resembles *tawatur*, the overwhelming agreement of multiply related reports that engenders certainty in the minds of those who learn of it. In order for the Muslim community to accept certain texts as authentic and therefore act upon them, the agreement of the community – either the community as a whole or its scholars – serves as a guarantor of correctness.

Both of these understandings, especially the first, exist in tension with his critique of consensus in the *Summation* and his treatment of the agreement of a particular community's scholars in his critiques of Malik. In the *Summation*, he disputes with his unnamed interlocutor about when the agreement of the scholars suffices to constitute consensus. How many is close enough to universal? What if one of them is absent, or dies, or changes his mind? These arguments were probably directed against Iraqi scholars including Abu Bakr al-Asamm (d. around 200/816–17) and Ibrahim ibn 'Ulayya, "infamous jurist-theologians whose jurisprudence was based on the primacy of consensus, even if only partial, at the expense of prophetic reports" (El Shamsy 2009, 53). For Shafi'i, neither the "consensus" of a group of scholars (as discussed in the *Summation*) nor the accepted practice of a community (i.e. the *'amal* of Medina) is adequate proof of a rule, since some dissent from these views, or could dissent without any facts having changed. To his mind, the claim of consensus only serves to justify arbitrary choices between one view and another. Disagreement itself is not the problem; we have seen that it is one acceptable result of *ijtihad*. But there, unlike with the claim of consensus by his opponents, there is a text to which one can refer back.

His preference for textual sources over broad agreement based on unknown or unverifiable evidence renders him willing – in another view disputed by his early opponents – to prefer isolated reports (*khabar al-wahid* or sometimes *khabar al-khassa*) from a Companion to views supported by human reason untethered to revealed texts. These reports, sometimes only on the authority of a single reliable individual, may be epistemologically shaky compared to those confirmed by *tawatur*, but acting upon them is acceptable.

A short work treats the divergent opinions attributed to two of the Prophet's Companions: *The Disagreements between 'Ali and 'Abdallah ibn Mas'ud*. The question of disagreement among the first generation of Muslims is important methodologically for Shafi'i. Companion traditions are of interest to him as a secondary resource — usable only when there is no acceptable prophetic sunna. But to adhere to the view of one Companion or group of Companions over another skirts too close to the ungrounded personal whim that he deplores in his rejection of Medinan customary practice and the "consensus" of Iraqi scholars.

These discussions of consensus and isolated reports in his works of legal theory and method highlight the importance of disputation and debate to the legal culture of the time, but also highlight both personal qualities of Shafi'i himself and the linkages between law and other fields of inquiry, including theology. His later biographers credit him with skills necessary to victory in contests of wits: eloquence, logic, mastery of texts. Bayhaqi devotes a forty-page chapter in his biography to "Shafi'i's excellence in debate and his overcoming by means of knowledge and evidence everyone who debated with him." Oral debates lent themselves to written elaboration: the exchanges with unnamed opponents over accepting hadith or relying on scholarly agreement were expanded far beyond what would be possible in purely extemporaneous debate. Yet the occasional and casuistic nature of the exchanges is clear and suggests that real exchanges formed the basis for the written works. The *Umm* likewise frequently adopts the framework of a discussion with a hypothetical interlocutor in order to display Shafi'i's ideas and persuasive arguments to best advantage. Even sections supposedly aimed at exposition rather than direct comparison of doctrines often take on an argumentative tone. Did Shafi'i borrow his debating strategies from theologians despite the fact that he is often said to have disapproved of theological speculation? This remains unclear. It is certainly the case, as Abu Zahra puts it, that "the general ambience was one of argumentation and disputation" (2001, 290).

LAW AND THEOLOGY

In the *Summation*, Shafi'i makes fairly frequent reference to "the theologians" (*ahl al-kalam*), though it is unclear precisely what he understands by this term – probably mostly the rationalist Muʿtazila. Much of what has been said about his theological views by later generations is back projection; there is no reason to suspect, for instance, that he had any interest in or position on the createdness or otherwise of the Qurʾan. He was not deeply engaged in debating the principal theological controversies of the time on the intertwined issues of human free will, predestination, and the nature of divine justice. "There is nothing more repellent to me," he reportedly said, "than theology (*kalam*) and its practitioners (*ahlihi*)" (Ibn Qadi Shubha 2003, 43). An anecdote tells us that after debating Hafs al-Fard, presumably in Egypt, he declared that he hated *kalam*. Yet this report also tells us that he engaged in disputation with people whom posterity knows as theologians (though Hafs is not usually identified as a Muʿtazili). This does not mean, of course, that their engagements necessarily focused on theological topics; Abu Bakr al-Asamm, for instance, also had views about consensus with which Shafiʿi disagreed vociferously.

The Muʿtazila were not the only practitioners of theology in the second/eighth century, but they were among the most important and influential, and those with whom Shafiʿi was most likely to have interacted. The movement originated with Wasil ibn ʿAtaʾ (d. 131/748) and, subsequently, ʿAmr ibn ʿUbayd (d. 144/761). Both men were students of al-Hasan al-Basri (d. 110/782), who rejected predestination and upheld human free will, stressing that people were entirely responsible for their own bad acts and God could in no sense be held accountable for human sins. Later classical definitions of Muʿtazilism stress a handful of doctrines, including God's absolute justice, the ability of human reason to discern good apart from revelation, and the existence of an objective Good with which God acts in accordance. The most famous doctrine associated with the Muʿtazila had to do with the debate over whether God had created the Qurʾan in time: was there a time when God was and the Qurʾan was not? The Abbasid caliph al-Maʾmun in 218/833 declared it imperative that scholars affirm the created nature of the Qurʾan, granting Muʿtazilism semi-official status. (Ibn Hanbal's reputation soared as a result of his refusal to capitulate despite imprisonment and torture.) Al-Mutawakkil lifted this decree in 234/848, and the resulting backlash boosted traditionalism.

Makdisi (1984, 11) says:

> by raising the Prophet's Sunna to the level of the Koran, and by restricting the use of analogical reasoning within definite limits, Shafi'i's purpose was to create for traditionalism a science which could be used as an antidote to *kalam*, another already well-established science associated with the rationalist Mu'tazila ... whom he regarded as his adversaries.

Yet Makdisi exaggerates Shafi'i's commitment to pure traditionalism. To be sure, Shafi'i refuses in typically traditionalist fashion to speculate about the nature of God's attributes. On other points, he undoubtedly expresses "anti-Mu'tazili" (Lowry 2007, 300) positions. Still, he neither argues for these views in standard dialectical terms nor does he refuse to engage entirely with them. Instead, he shifts the terms of the debate. Lowry argues that the *Risala* constitutes, in its own way, a theological polemic. Shafi'i was predestinarian in an atypical way, making the unique claim that "God has predetermined ... the way in which He has structured the law" and that "there is no escaping that foreordained legal architecture" (2007, 307). Shafi'i links divine foreknowledge and predestination specifically to the structure of the law: God knows in advance which obligations will be imposed on His creatures permanently, which will eventually be abrogated, and that some will be imposed through Muhammad's legislative activity. God even ordained that people would sometimes need to engage in *ijtihad*. The upshot of all of this is that Shafi'i presents his own description of the structure of the law as preordained by God – in fact, "as theologically inescapable" (Lowry 2007, 311).

Shafi'i saw an organic connection between revelation, God's sovereignty, and the nature of humanity's relationship to God. Despite his expressed distaste for theological disputation, he held indisputably theological ideas. It should be no surprise that these, for him, were closely connected to the law and God's purposeful legislative activity. The discipline of jurisprudence, *fiqh*, was necessary, but strict limits on human reasoning prevented anyone straying over the line into legislating: God alone is lawgiver.

Eventually, in the aftermath of the Inquisition (*mihna*), an oppositional theological school centered on the thought of Abu'l-Hasan al-Ash'ari (d. 324/935) would triumph. Nasr Hamid Abu Zayd (2007) has identified al-Ash'ari along with Shafi'i and the later al-Ghazali (d. 505/1111) as three voices of a dominant Sunni synthesis which has come to be taken for granted, rather than viewed as the product of human endeavor. Its presuppositions are widely perceived as unchallengeable and unchangeable. Some have held that, although it had a far broader impact, Ash'arism had a special relationship with Shafi'i jurisprudence; they melded to form what Melchert (2004) has called a "compromise, semi-rationalist" school. A few later Shafi'i jurists of note belonged to other theological tendencies but they are notable in part because of their rarity. On the other hand, Chaumont has suggested that this is an exaggeration: the vast majority of Shafi'is may have been Ash'aris, but the same was true of other Sunnis.

5

THE *UMM* AND SUBSTANTIVE LAW

Shafi'i may be known primarily for his work on legal theory, but his compendium of substantive law comprises the bulk of the written work attributed to him. Shafi'i's writings on hermeneutics can help in understanding his substantive jurisprudence. Both types of work return repeatedly to themes of prophetic exemplariness, the coherence of revelation, the importance of language, and the necessity for specialist expertise in interpretation. They also reveal something of the man behind the works, especially his intellectual preoccupations and perfectionist temperament. His insistence on methodological consistency sometimes leads him to highly counterintuitive rules. In part, this emphasis can be explained by his continual engagement in disputation. In ongoing polemics, one must espouse positions susceptible to logical defense even when taken to absurd ends. Whether his predilection for consistency made him a good debater or his taste for debate reinforced his mania for logic, the role of scholarly exchange (or heated dispute) in refining legal arguments and doctrines is a critical element differentiating Shafi'i from someone like Ibn Hanbal. Nowhere is this clearer than in Shafi'i's magnum opus, the *Kitab al-Umm*, variously translated as the *Exemplar*, the *Foundation*, the *Source*, or the *Motherbook*. The positive legal doctrines expressed, justified, and defended against criticism in its pages show both Shafi'i's genius and his deep situatedness in the legal discussions of his time.

TEXTUAL HISTORY OF THE *UMM*

The *Umm* has a more complicated history than the *Risala*. It comprises several layers of material with differing degrees of polish. Several recent works have attempted to trace its history and ascribe its elements to Shafi'i and the generations of students after him. Calder, who also questioned the dating and the attribution of the *Risala*, argued on the basis of formal criteria applied to the text itself that the *Umm* was substantially later than usually suggested. More hermeneutically sophisticated arguments, he claimed, came later, and thus the less sophisticated arguments attributed to Shafi'i's student Rabi' ibn Sulayman al-Muradi represented the earliest segments of the text.

Calder's scholarship has spurred renewed investigation of the early textual tradition across the legal schools. Working on the basis of quotations of the *Umm* in manuscript works of the following generation or two, Ahmed El Shamsy has shown that not only do the doctrines in the *Umm* generally go back to Shafi'i himself, but the words of the text were largely fixed sometime during the third/ninth century. Over a dozen late third/ninth- and early fourth/tenth-century works, mostly by scholars who studied with Rabi', quote the *Umm* both extensively and accurately. A treatise on legal disagreements by Rabi''s student Abu Bakr ibn al-Mundhir (d. 318/930) contains around four hundred such quotations, and a single quotation in a slightly earlier text on prayer by Muhammad ibn Nasr al-Marwazi (d. 294/907) runs to over three hundred words.

Of course, a fixed text does not guarantee that the words in the text are those of the master. Inevitably, there has been debate about the extent to which the text faithfully reproduces Shafi'i's own words. This is not an exclusively modern concern; at least one fourth/tenth-century scholar alleged that Buwayti authored the *Umm*. Modern scholars who attribute the text to Shafi'i nonetheless disagree about what precisely that means. Melchert argues that the phrase "Shafi'i said," which introduces many statements in the *Umm*, can mean a range of things: "Shafi'i said (in my hearing)," "Shafi'i said (in someone else's hearing)," "Shafi'i wrote," "an adherent of Shafi'i said," and "if Shafi'i were here to answer our questions, I am sure he would say." And in each case, the formula might imply a paraphrase rather than verbatim transmission (Melchert 2004, 297).

El Shamsy (in a forthcoming article) counters, though, that the *Umm* frequently specifies the way in which its information was transmitted to Shafi'i, and from him to his audience. This ought to inspire more confidence in the reliability of the text and its concern with precise attribution. For instance, some of the text as it currently exists has Rabi' reporting on Buwayti's authority rather than that of Shafi'i himself. (Rabi' used to run errands for Shafi'i and would need corroboration for any portion of a lecture that he missed; protocol required direct audition.) Evidence overwhelmingly supports El Shamsy's contentions that the *Umm* is based on lecture notes compiled by Rabi' and his numerous students, that its contents accurately reflect Shafi'i's views and words, and that it has been preserved, save "occasional copyist mistakes," in essentially the form it was composed.

CAREER OF THE *UMM*

Although the *Umm* contains Shafi'i's doctrines and was transmitted, apparently quite accurately, to a number of early Shafi'i scholars it did not long remain a primary legal manual for Shafi'i scholars. Epitomes produced by Muzani and Buwayti quickly supplanted the *Umm* as teaching resources. The "daunting length" – El Shamsy counts 6500 pages – and scattershot organization of the *Umm* were doubtless key factors. Buwayti abridged it to 200 pages in his *Digest*, which quickly spread both west to Andalusia and east as far as Bukhara. Muzani's *Digest* spawned numerous commentaries, and became a central part of the curriculum of the emerging Shafi'i school; it was ultimately far more influential than the *Umm* itself in the establishment of distinctively Shafi'i doctrines. Authoritative compendia produced in later centuries rendered the *Umm* obsolete. It is only since the publication of the Bulaq edition at the outset of the twentieth century that the *Umm* has reemerged as a vital text, now for historians rather than jurists. (That said, some Indonesian religious scholars have taken up the study of the master's works.) Modern editions of the *Umm* usually run to seven or eight volumes, including several brief treatises like the ones mentioned in the previous chapter; the newest edition has eleven volumes. Despite its antiquarian rather than doctrinal importance, the *Umm* has become a very important book in early Islamic legal studies.

The bulk of the *Umm* is devoted to consideration of specific legal issues. Its subject matter proceeds from matters of ritual purity and worship (prayer, alms, fasting, pilgrimage) to hunting and dietary rules to pecuniary transactions with social effects (or the reverse, social transactions with pecuniary effects): sales, pledges, preemption, gifts, foundlings, and inheritance — both fixed shares and legacies. Relations with non-Muslims are regulated, from calculating the poll tax to slaughtering livestock while fighting in enemy territory to marrying women from the People of the Book. This last topic recurs in the section on marriage, which is followed by divorce and then miscellaneous oaths of abstinence, their consequences, and the means by which they may be expiated. Other sections deal with criminal punishments, fines for injuries, and rules of evidence. Also in the mix are rules for the support of children, the manumission of slaves, and the proper way to carry a funeral litter.

HERMENEUTICAL STRATEGIES

Several characteristics distinguish the *Umm*'s treatment of substantive points: a careful parsing of revealed texts, a concern to address diverse variables affecting judgments, and a propensity to engage in disputation with named or anonymous representatives of diverging opinions. These characteristics are uneven, however. Some sections are more concerned to lay out logic, others to interpret specific passages of revelation, still others to argue disputed points. Throughout, Shafi'i's willingness to engage in hypothetical speculation about legal issues, rather than limit himself to pronouncing on concrete issues – things that actually happened – sets him apart from hadith scholars like Ibn Hanbal.

The *Umm* generally follows the methodological principles Shafi'i lays out in his *Risala*: grounding doctrines in the revealed sources. Where he can, Shafi'i draws support for his views first from Qur'an and then hadith. He usually quotes hadith with a chain of transmitters. He is particularly careful to do so where he knows of dispute about a specific topic. His detractors pointed out that, despite his insistence on high standards for proof texts, the hadith he cited did not always meet the bar. This was a significant enough accusation that his biographer Bayhaqi marshals evidence to refute it.

Where no relevant Qur'anic passage exists, he simply begins with hadith. For instance, with regard to the question of the imam pausing during his Friday sermon to address a remark to someone, Shafi'i adduces a hadith in which two Companions relate that "a man entered the mosque while the Messenger of God was at the pulpit. He (i.e. Muhammad) asked: have you prayed? He said: No. He said: Pray two *rakats*." Shafi'i states, implicitly relying on the notion that the Prophet's act sets precedent, that "there is no harm in a man speaking during a Friday sermon." Moreover, regardless of whether such speech is permissible or discouraged, it does not invalidate either his sermon or his subsequent prayer (*Umm* 1:345). (His student Yunus ibn 'Abd al-A'la notes, without referring to any prophetic precedent, that Shafi'i held that if a man sneezes during prayer, "there is no harm in [another] worshipper saying 'God bless you'" [IAH 283]. Note that this is a case where Shafi'i is said to have changed his mind; he previously held that one ought not to utter the customary formula to a sneezer; Muzani treats the shift in his *Digest*.) His remarks show concern for consistency and the ways that rules of social etiquette intersect with and must be reconciled with guidelines for valid worship.

In other instances, Shafi'i takes Qur'an and sunna for granted and focuses on elaboration of scripture rather than exegetical interpretation. Take the case of expiation of an oath (specifically, *zihar*) by fasting (*Umm* 5:407). Shafi'i alludes to the Qur'anic verse (58:4) which commands daytime fasting for two sequential months but proceeds to an extended discussion of how one counts those months. Any fast interrupted, for a legitimate reason or not, must be started over: days already fasted do not count. The Prophet forbade fasting on five specific days, including the two Eids; if any of these days fall within the chosen period, one must also begin anew. If one begins fasting at the sighting of the new moon, one proceeds for two lunar months precisely, whether that ends up being fifty-eight, fifty-nine, or sixty days. However, if one starts in the middle of a month, one fasts the rest of that month, keeping track of how many days one fasts. One then fasts the next lunar month in its entirety. In the following month, one makes up however many days are necessary to complete thirty from the partial first month. One might consider this detailed enumeration of possible scenarios unimportant – or perhaps indicative of someone suffering from some sort of compulsive disorder. To Shafi'i, however, the point is that the law provides a mechanism for addressing each and every query, no matter how niggling, that a believer might have. The devil is most decidedly not in the details: holiness is. Of course, the calculation of two months is not the only factor at issue. Shafi'i proceeds to discuss intention and other matters with the same scrupulous attention to minutiae.

THE *UMM*'S JURISPRUDENCE IN COMPARATIVE VIEW

The *Umm* engages revealed texts systematically. Shafi'i carefully parses texts to yield even obvious answers, demonstrating his delight in logic for its own sake and the coherence of revelation. The deeply exegetical nature of the *Umm*'s approach stands out when it is juxtaposed to other texts of its time. A brief comparison of how three texts discuss a simple point regarding dower (a payment a husband makes, or debt he incurs, to his wife at the time of marriage) brings these differences into relief. The point, on which all agree, is that failure to settle the dower amount at the time of contract does not void the marriage. I begin with the Maliki *Mudawwana* and move to the *Kitab al-Hujja*, Shaybani's polemic against Medinan views, before discussing the *Umm*.

A Qur'anic passage is the background for these legal discussions of dower. It states:

> There is no blame on you if you divorce women when you have not touched them or fixed their portions (*farida*). Give them [something], the wealthy according to his capacity and the poor according to his capacity, an equitable gift, a duty on those who do what is right. And if you divorce them before you have touched them but after fixing their portions, then half of what you have fixed for them, unless they forgive it or the one in whose hand is the marriage tie forgives it. Forgiving is nearer to piety. And do not forget generosity between yourselves, for God sees all that you do.
>
> (Q. 2:236–7)

These verses form the background against which the *Mudawwana* pursues the topic. The *Mudawwana* is a Maliki legal text, comparable in scope to the *Umm*, in which Sahnun al-Tanukhi, a Maliki who resided in Egypt during the decade prior to Shafi'i's arrival there, asks Malik's disciple Ibn al-Qasim questions about Malik's views and those of other Medinan authorities:

> [Sahnun] said: What if a man marries a woman and does not specify a dower for her? [Ibn al-Qasim] said: The marriage is allowed, according to Malik. He provides her with her fair dower, according to Malik, if he consummates [the marriage]. If he divorces her before they mutually agree on a dower then she is due a gift, and if he dies before they mutually agree on a dower she is due neither a gift nor a dower, but she is due inheritance.
>
> (Sahnun b. Sa'id al-Tanukhi 1905–1906, 2:238)

That Ibn al-Qasim had the Qur'anic passage in mind is obvious in the way he links consummation, payment of the full dower, the question of whether a dower has been fixed, and divorce. The Qur'an never directly addresses the validity of a marriage where the marriage portion or dower goes unspecified, nor does it set a consequence if consummation transpires without a dower having been fixed. The *Mudawwana* gives Malik's views on both points. Ibn al-Qasim implicitly refers to those rules the Qur'an does provide as he moves from responding to Sahnun's query to adducing additional rules that flow from the verses in question.

In a handful of texts, Abu Hanifa's disciples Shaybani and Abu Yusuf agree with their Maliki counterparts that lack of a fixed dower does not invalidate the marriage. What makes a comparison between the *Mudawwana* and the *Hujja* interesting is Shaybani's insistence on relating the marriage's validity to a larger legal topic, something the *Mudawwana* ignores. As he targets the views of Malik and his associates, Shaybani links the question of lack of fixed dower in a marriage contract to the larger problem of contracts with unspecified compensation:

> If a man marries a woman and does not fix a dower for her, the marriage is permitted and she is due her fair dower calculated according to her female relatives; it is neither decreased nor increased. But if it were a sale or some other type of lease or hire and a man purchased [something] without a price or leased [something] without a fixed compensation, that is not permitted.
> (Shaybani 1965, 3:215)

Unlike his counterparts, Shafi'i considers it necessary to prove, not merely assert, the validity of a marriage where dower has not been settled. He derives his proof step by step from the Qur'an. The relevant verses address two distinct situations when divorce takes place before consummation. If one divorces a woman whom one has not touched *before* setting her dower she must be given a gift. If one divorces a woman whom one has not touched *after* doing so, then she gets half the specified amount. His case hinges on a word:

the Qur'an uses the term "divorce" in both cases. Since "divorce" only applies to a wife, both women must be wives; therefore the first marriage must be valid even though no dower was set. One can almost hear the smug "Ta da!" (In the *Risala* [174] he makes a different argument, relevant to his concern with prohibitions in that portion of the text: sex with a woman is forbidden except for when specific conditions are attained; dower is not one of those conditions and so it is not required for a valid marriage.)

Shafi'i's concerns in the *Umm*, though, are not merely for the proper understanding of scripture. Were it so, it would be hard to explain why Shafi'i makes explicit a logical progression that everyone understands implicitly in order to justify a position no one disagrees with. Instead, his method here illuminates his broader aim: to connect rules derivable from clear revealed texts with broader legal-methodological principles. In particular, he seeks to find consistency between types of problems where one normally can apply analogical reasoning. Legal reasoning is not merely applying discrete rules but also seeking patterns. In this case, he must justify a divergence between the rule necessitated by the Qur'anic text and the more usual process of thinking about dower, which proceeds on the basis of an analogy to a sale. Although Shafi'i "generally applies rules for sales to marriage," Q. 2:236 carves out an exception. A marriage is valid even when the dower is not fixed in advance, but a sale without an agreed upon purchase price is not valid: "A marriage differs in this way from a sale, because if a sale occurs without a price it is not binding" (*Umm* 5:105). This need to explain a departure from an expected fit between substantive rules and broad principles is what makes him a legal theorist and not merely a jurist.

When the *Umm* tackles competing views explicitly, jurisprudential method sometimes comes to the fore, but the tactics adopted can vary considerably when it shifts from straightforward explication of Shafi'i's positions to implicit or explicit contrast with the views of named or unnamed opponents. For instance, one brief section coming at the heels of a discussion of damaged property in invalid sales treats the case of a raped or coerced woman. Shafi'i holds that neither a free woman nor a female slave should be punished in any way. The man in question, however, will be subject to the appropriate fixed punishment for illicit sex (stoning if married, lashing and banishment if unmarried), as well as being obligated to pay compensation to the free woman or the slave's master. Shaybani, in contrast, advocates only compensatory payment which obviates the possibility of punishment: one cannot have both payment and punishment for the same act. In dissenting, the *Umm* does not quote any Qur'anic text or prophetic tradition. Rather, the discussion revolves around whether the precedent of a Medinan Companion serves as proof. Shafi'i thinks that it does, while Shaybani holds otherwise. This position accords with Shafi'i's preference for the isolated view of a Companion over a jurist's deductions. But the lack of explicit textual arguments can also be explained as a survival from his earlier modes of argument: it parallels a section in his *Refutation of Muhammad ibn al-Hasan* [*Shaybani*], written when he still identified as a disciple of Malik.

LEGAL DISAGREEMENT AND SHAFI'I'S SHORT TREATISES

Differences of opinion played a significant role among early jurists in general, and for Shafi'i in particular, given his shifting allegiances and eclectic training. Much of his career involved exploring differences of opinion in oral disputation and in written form. Although the *Umm* deals fairly extensively with legal differences, its primary function is as a compendium of Shafi'i's legal ideas. Legal differences are given attention in various topical subdivisions of the *Umm*, sometimes in passing, sometimes in sustained form. They are implicit as a backdrop. The *Umm*'s discussions by default intervene in ongoing debates. Often, the disagreements remain implicit and the *Umm* focuses merely on elucidating Shafi'i's views and presenting their supporting evidence. In other cases, though, the text tackles disagreements explicitly. On some issues, even once Shafi'i has clearly broken with Malik's method, he upholds Malik's position against Hanafi critics. In such cases, the *Umm* defends Malik's ruling by citing scriptural authority and/or building, inference by inference, a case for it. In other cases, Shafi'i agrees with the Hanafi doctrine, though seldom characterizing it as such. Again, though, the rationales and proofs he provides often differ substantially. On yet other occasions, Shafi'i's doctrines depart from those held by either group of jurists, and he points out the pitfalls of both. This usually occurs in cases where Shafi'i considers the Maliki view illogical and the Hanafi view whimsical and insufficiently grounded in revelation.

Shafi'i's jurisprudence in the *Umm* is often sympathetic to Malik's substantive positions but critical of his methodology. He operates constructively to buttress Medinan views with scriptural evidence that Malik never felt obliged to provide. He does so in response to Hanafi criticism — often explicit in Hanafi works of disagreement and criticism, such as the version of Malik's *Muwatta'* reported by Shaybani which intersperses Malik's views with Abu Hanifa's views, and the *Hujja* also attributed to Shaybani. Although it is not clear whether Shafi'i had access to any version of this compilation (the attribution to Shaybani is by no means certain), he would certainly have been familiar with both its specific doctrines and its general argumentative techniques.

Such differences are treated more explicitly and extensively in a number of short works dealing more or less exclusively with substantive and methodological disagreements between early legal authorities. They vary in tone from dispassionately comparative to violently polemical. The topics covered in these treatises again run the gamut from ritual to commercial matters. The three longest sections of the *Disagreements between the Two Iraqis*, for instance, focus on debts, divorce, and dates — specifically, selling unripe dates. The amount of space devoted to various topics does not necessarily reflect their significance in Muslim life, but rather the extent to which the legal issues involve interesting methodological differences.

Three treatises written at different times show Shafi'i entangled in networks of jurisprudential conversation and controversy. The *Refutation of Muhammad ibn al-Hasan [Shaybani]* has a distinctly Maliki tone. *Disagreements between the Two Iraqis (Ikhtilaf al-Iraqiyayn*, sometimes read "Iraqiyyin" in the plural, not dual) reproduces, with Shafi'i's commentary, a text by Abu Yusuf comparing the doctrines of Abu Hanifa with his Kufan contemporary and rival Ibn Abi Layla. The commentary in the text displays growing independence from other authorities' views. *Disagreements between Malik and Shafi'i* was composed by Rabi' and depicts Shafi'i's harshest rejection of what he saw as the methodological failings of Malik and his followers.

Another treatise by Abu Yusuf is also preserved with Shafi'i's commentary. Just as *Two Iraqis* compares Ibn Abi Layla's views with Abu Hanifa's views, followed by Shafi'i's commentary, the *Siyar al-Awza'i* presents (Abu Yusuf's rendering of) Abu Hanifa's views in contrast to those of the Syrian scholar al-Awza'i (d. 157/774) with Shafi'i's frequently dissenting commentary. How war and conquest were to be conducted and subject populations dealt with preoccupied Iraqi jurists extensively, since the seat of empire had moved there. The Syrian Awza'i had dealt with the topic in detail, Damascus having been the seat of the Umayyads. (Shaybani not only transmitted Abu Yusuf's text to Shafi'i but composed one of his own. Shaybani's own *Siyar* has been translated by Khadduri as *The Islamic Law of Nations*.) These two treatises preserving Abu Yusuf's dialogue with other jurists of his time reflect both the knowledge of Iraqi jurisprudence that Shafi'i gained from his study there and also his critical distance from those views. (Shafi'i never seems to have traveled to Syria or to have engaged its jurists in any significant way.)

The *Invalidation of Juristic Preference* (*Ibtal al-Istihsan*, a composite document, not an authored essay) takes direct aim at the legal technique whereby a jurist overrides an obvious ruling in favor of another due to considerations outside the strict scope of analogy. Juristic preference is similar to, although more restricted in scope than, "*istislah*," which means picking one ruling because of its anticipated benefits for society or the welfare of a given group. Shafi'i also objected to juristic preference in the *Invalidation* and the *Risala*. He thought it self-indulgent. More problematic, it meant departing from revealed texts, since juristic preference would come into play either where, on the one hand, there was no explicit scriptural text nor a clear logical link to one or, on the other hand, where the text or its derivative ruling was unpalatable. Mohammad Hashim Kamali (1991) points out the theological problem that this posed for Shafi'i: to suggest a lack of clear guidance in a given situation implied a shortcoming in God's revelation, which encompasses everything, while to ignore God's guidance in favor of a solution based on human whim implied unthinkable hubris.

DISTINCTIVE DOCTRINES: LITERALISM OR "PLAIN SENSE" INTERPRETATION

Muslim scholars have always been preoccupied by the interpretation of texts. Given that words — Arabic words especially — can signify multiple things, both literal and allusive, understanding their meaning in specific instances is of paramount importance. In particular, the Qur'an has traditionally been held to deliver more than one level of meaning. But where its verses have legal implications, the apparent plain meaning of its words takes precedence in Shafi'i's view. (Of course "apparent" meaning may be in the eye of the beholder.) Although Shafi'i does not practice the austere literalism that Dawud al-Zahiri comes to support two generations later, his plain-sense interpretation of some terms is striking.

One of these is the reading of the word "touch" in the Qur'anic verses (4:43 and 5:6) pertaining to ablution, the ritual purification before required prayers. Ablution is necessary, the Qur'an states, "if you have touched (*lamasa*) women." What kind of touch is meant? Since the Qur'an only speaks of sex indirectly, Abu Hanifa understood "touch" here as a euphemism for intercourse; sex cancels ritual purity but ordinary touching does not. Malik took the slightly broader view that the term means any touching with lustful intent (or arousing result); non-sexual touching does not qualify. Shafi'i, however, holds that one must interpret a term literally unless there is strong reason to do otherwise. Thus, like several early Companions, he takes the position that skin to skin contact between a man and a woman who is not one of his close relations nullifies ablution. (Rabi' recalls that when asked about touching, Shafi'i made reference to the Prophet's stance on *mulamasa*, a related word which refers to touching fabric when buying it; he also quoted a line of poetry.)

Shafi'i has a similarly absolutist understanding of another rule. His quirky interpretation of paternity in cases of illegitimacy sheds light on several dynamics of his legal thought: his insistence on logical consistency, his recourse to texts, his willingness to address hypothetical cases, and his willingness to distinguish between valid and virtuous actions. Muslim authorities unanimously hold that children born of illicit relations have no legal father. Bastards do not take their natural fathers' names, inherit from them, or have legal obligations toward or claims upon them. As a matter of law no filial relationship exists. Thus, Shafi'i concludes logically, a man may contract a valid marriage with a female child born from his own illicit liaison: offspring from a forbidden tryst is not (legally) his progeny. One cannot have things both ways: either she is his daughter, in which case the legal rulings attached to paternity apply, or she is not, in which case they do not. Apart from a few Malikis who agree with Shafi'i on this point, other groups of jurists have uniformly rejected his conclusion. Ibn Hanbal is willing to grant the premise that a paternity decision may require a certain legal verdict, but one must still act in accordance with the *actual* state of things. Shafi'i's commitment to logic, and perhaps to holding positions that could hold up in debate when pressed to their logical conclusions, leads him to formulate a logically unassailable but nonetheless absurd position.

THE SHAFI'I SCHOOL

Shafi'i did not found a legal school, nor did his direct students. That honor goes to Abu'l-'Abbas ibn Surayj (d. 306/918) and his Baghdadi colleagues. However, a circle – or rather, circles – of students and their students proceeding in Shafi'i's way certainly existed from Shafi'i's death onward. They contested his legacy; like most transfers of power, it was bumpy. Some of the conflict was over principles and some was personal. Among Shafi'i's key disciples were a few potential leaders, including Muzani, Buwayti, and Ibn 'Abd al-Hakam's son Muhammad ibn 'Abdallah, now known as a Maliki. One account declares that, rather than simply having had a change of heart due to legal principles, Muhammad ibn 'Abdallah was a contender to take over the circle after Shafi'i's death. Upon losing to Buwayti, however, he reasserted his Maliki loyalties and composed a refutation of Shafi'i's views. Despite this defection, Ibn Qadi Shubha includes a notice for him in his dictionary of Shafi'i jurists because he transmits some of Shafi'i's legal views. Others pointedly exclude him.

Lingering resentments and tensions may have led Muzani and Harmala (along with one of Shafi'i's sons) to "denounce" Buwayti to the Inquisition which would erupt in the decade after Shafi'i's death, when the caliph required scholars to confess belief in the createdness of the Qur'an. Buwayti's ultimate death in a Baghdad prison can be explained without reference to intrigue by rivals, though. As El Shamsy notes, a new provincial administration in Egypt had overturned the Maliki-dominated officialdom, and targeted non-Hanafis for persecution. Buwayti stressed the scriptural rather than systematic element: "I heard Shafi'i say: If I say something and there is a sound statement from the Messenger of God to the contrary, then my view (*qawli*) is what the Messenger of God said" (Subki 1999, 1:382). Muzani stressed instead the master's jurisprudential techniques, considering himself both capable of and justified in addressing new questions by applying the same procedures Shafi'i had used in other cases, rather than deciding every new case on the basis of reference to scriptural texts. Had Buwayti lived as long as Muzani and Rabi', who survived Shafi'i by, respectively, fifty-seven and sixty-four years, it is possible the school would have looked quite different.

Among those who studied with both Muzani and Rabi' was Abu'l-Qasim 'Uthman ibn Sa'id al-Anmati (d. 288/901), who was in turn the teacher of Abu'l-'Abbas ibn Surayj. Ibn Surayj, who displayed a flair for legal theory, served for a time as a judge in Shiraz but is best known for teaching and disputation: he debated with Muhammad, the son of Dawud al-Zahiri, and with the Hanafi 'Isa ibn Aban. Through these ongoing polemical activities Shafi'i's ideas continued to reverberate, but with growth and refinements to keep them competitive in the marketplace of ideas.

From the circles of Egyptian disciples, passing through Baghdad via Ibn Surayj and others, the Shafi'i legal school came to hold sway over much of the Middle East. The fortunes of the Shafi'i school waxed and waned in Egypt. Suppressed in favor of Hanafism during the period shortly after Shafi'i's life, it flourished under the regime of Ahmad ibn Tulun and his descendants (r. 254–92/868–905). From Egypt, Shafi'ism spread eastward. Monique Bernards and John Nawas (2003) find that in Iraq during the period 251–400, only one-tenth of Iraqi jurists were Shafi'is. (A similar fraction was Maliki; over half were Hanbalis.) Shafi'ism lagged behind Malikism everywhere except in the East (including Transoxiana and Khurasan), where it came to constitute a slim majority. The Ayyubid era saw a resurgence of Shafi'ism, which was patronized by powerful sultans, not only in Egypt but in Syria and elsewhere. The medieval practice of having four official schools, with a judge from each appointed in major cities, meant that Shafi'ism had a key presence even when it was a minority tradition; under Mamluk rule, the shift to appointing a chief judge from each school diminished Shafi'i preeminence. Later, the official Hanafism of the Ottoman empire and then India's Mughal rulers led to that school claiming the largest share of the Sunni populace, which it still maintains. Nonetheless, Shafi'ism has retained a powerful presence even in lands once ruled by Ottomans. Today, it has a strong foothold in parts of the Middle East (Yemen, Oman, and Bahrain though not the Hijaz), parts of Syria and Egypt (mostly southern and rural), East Africa, and – circuitously – Southeast Asia, where it claims the allegiance of nearly all Sunni Muslims in populous Indonesia and Malaysia.

Shafi'ism has historically had more than its share of intellectual superstars. Within the Sunni tradition, the compilers of the canonical hadith collections as well as Muhyi al-Din Abu Zakariyya Yahya al-Nawawi (d. 676/1277), the theologian Abu'l-Hasan al-Ash'ari, "Imam al-Haramayn" al-Juwayni (478/1085), and the polymath al-Ghazali (d. 505/1111) were Shafi'is. The school has also maintained a relatively strong network of scholars, despite the challenges that colonialism and its aftermath posed to traditional educational institutions. Egypt's al-Azhar, the premier institution of Sunni learning, has a Shafi'i scholar at its head. One of al-Azhar's graduates, Egypt's "Mufti of the Republic" since 2003, 'Ali Gum'a (b. 1952) is a Shafi'i (and a Shadhili Sufi). Known as a bit of a renegade, he is nonetheless widely respected for his erudition.

Traditional scholarship has faced two major challenges in the last two centuries. First, nation states have reduced religious law's jurisdiction to matters of family and, sometimes, a handful of criminal or charitable provisions, and have shifted to codified law rather than jurists' law. Second, the Salafi revivalist movement has termed the legal schools and the body of scholarship they have produced an innovation, a departure from strict reliance on pure revealed texts. One response has been a surge in new traditionalism, using new media and methods, including online classes teaching traditional texts and subsidized translations of classic works of scholarship. One of the best-known Shafi'i scholars is American convert Nuh Ha Mim Keller, who has translated both a small work on ritual obligations (Nawawi's *Maqasid*) and a larger medieval reference work, *Reliance of the Traveler*.

If one is to measure Shafi'i's impact, though, even more crucial than the success of the legal school has been the infiltration of his methodological presuppositions and notions about scripture into the Sunni tradition as a whole. Though he was not responsible for the canonical "four source" theory of the law textbooks credit him with inventing, his ideas nonetheless transformed the trajectory of Sunni thinking not only about law but also about sunna, about language, and about God.

Image 1 The exterior of Shafi'i's mausoleum, probably photographed during the second quarter of the twentieth century. Copyright Creswell Archive, Ashmolean Museum, Image courtesy of Special Collections, Fine Arts Library, Harvard College Library.

6

SAINT SHAFI'I

As a young student, Palestinian-born Khayr al-Din al-Ramli (1585–1670/1) had doubts about his life's path. Inclined toward study of the law, he traveled to Cairo to study at al-Azhar. He was drawn to the Shafi'i legal school but his brother, with whom he was traveling, pushed him toward Hanafi jurisprudence instead. Hanafism had official status within the flourishing Ottoman empire and offered a reasonably lucrative career path. Torn, Khayr al-Din sought the counsel of a local scholar who advised him to seek Shafi'i's guidance. Khayr al-Din composed a letter asking Shafi'i's advice about which course of study he should pursue and carried it to his mausoleum. After placing it at the tomb he took a nap there. While he slept, Shafi'i visited him in a dream and informed him "We are all on the straight path" (quoted in Tucker 2001, 13). Khayr al-Din pragmatically chose Hanafi law, where he rose to prominence. His collection of legal opinions is still consulted today.

Khayr al-Din was but one of Shafi'i's many thousands of posthumous visitors. Visits to Shafi'i's tomb began well before Khayr al-Din and continue to the present day. Pilgrims request his intercession in their personal affairs, seeking his assistance with the trivial and tragic trials of daily existence. They bask in the tomb's aura of sanctity and soak up *baraka* or "blessing," the transmissible spiritual energy that emanates from holy places and people, living or dead. They recite the Qur'an and touch the massive carved wooden screen fitted over an acrylic glass box guarding Shafi'i's cenotaph. Visitors walk around the enclosure, stand at Shafi'i's feet

Image 2 One visitor makes supplication beside Shafi'i's cenotaph while another performs the prayer facing Mecca. The marble column marks the location of Shafi'i's head. Image courtesy of Mohamad S. Ali.

to make extended supplication, or perform ritual prayer at a niche in the mausoleum's corner. (This niche is newer than others built into the walls; the original builder miscalculated the direction of Mecca.) Although Friday is the day most associated with visits to Shafi'i's tomb, a recent Tuesday morning found a steady stream of male and female visitors, Egyptian and Southeast Asian. In addition to prayer, supplication, and circumambulation, one visitor was intent on videotaping the entire experience.

Like Khayr al-Din in the seventeenth century, Shafi'i's visitors sometimes bring letters, and some who cannot visit find other ways to deliver them. Even though one's physical presence at the tomb is the best way to absorb its blessing, sending letters by post or with a trusted proxy must sometimes suffice. Two scholars have studied Shafi'i's correspondence: Sayyid 'Uways in the 1960s and Emad Adly in the 1990s. In the mid-twentieth century, public scribes were available near the tomb, but today most supplicants handwrite their own letters; a few are typed on paper with a business letterhead. Nearly all letter-writers are adults; of those whose gender was discernible Adly found far more women than men (forty-seven per cent to twenty-seven per cent), though decades earlier 'Uways found that slightly over half were male (122 men to 110 women). The letters arrive in envelopes addressed variously to "The Tomb of Imam Shafi'i" or "Master Imam the Shariah Judge – Cairo" or "Master Imam Shafi'i in Egypt". Adly estimates that about fifty letters each week arrived by post or were delivered by hand at the tomb complex during his six months of fieldwork. Adly watched one "peasant [pull] out of his bundle a number of letters from other inhabitants of his village, al-Sharqiyya, and conscientiously pu[sh] them in one by one through the wooden balustrade surrounding Shafi'i's tomb, while reciting verses from Surat Yasin" (Adly 2008, 127). Letters, and the occasional photo, cluster at the corners where visitors slip them in through gaps in the protective box.

Though separated by decades, most of the letters resemble each other in their plaints. Some seek relief and other seek redress or revenge. In addition to numerous requests for the cessation of unspecified hardship, petitioners plead for Shafi'i to intercede on their behalf to obtain some benefit, like finding work, or to stop some harm, like infertility, spirit possession, the evil eye, or sorcery. 'Uways found one letter seeking the destruction of Israel. A more recent writer combines requests for relief and vengeance: extrication from a sticky romantic entanglement and harsh punishment of the temptress who led him astray. Shafi'i's proximity to God makes divine intervention possible: "I am submitting my complaint to he who is closer to God than I or any other. I submit my complaint to my lord the honourable and venerable imam, my lord Imam Shafi'i, may God approve of him" (Adly 2008, 128).

The roles of intercessor and judge overlap. Writers often address Shafi'i as judge or "the judge of Islamic law" or "the chief judge." They do not necessarily ask him to rule on the merits of particular cases or decide on consequences (petitioners frequently know precisely what ought to happen to their enemies), but to pronounce and enforce his verdicts. Though he never held a judgeship during his life, he is said by some of his devotees to sit with Husayn and Sayyida Zaynab, both 'Alid saints with important shrines in Cairo, "on the 'hidden court' (*mahkama batiniyya*), which determines the affairs of humans" (Hoffmann-Ladd 1992, 626). Adly puts it slightly differently: supplicants model "supernatural justice" on this-worldly institutional practices of courts.

In addition to regular visits to Shafi'i's tomb to seek his blessing or assistance, his devotees celebrate an annual birthday (*mawlid*) festival, usually on the first Wednesday of the lunar month of Sha'ban. *Mawlid* celebrations, first and foremost that of the Prophet, have historically been widespread throughout the Muslim world. Local saintly figures have also been widely celebrated in this fashion. With increasing controversy surrounding such birthday festivals, as well as (in the Egyptian case) reduced state support, it is notable that Shafi'i's continues to be celebrated as those of other saintly figures have been minimized or eliminated. How, though, did Shafi'i become a saintly figure, with a major mosque-*madrasa*-mausoleum complex dedicated to him, an annual celebration, regular traffic in pilgrims, and a reputation as an intercessor with God? Shafi'i became a symbol of Sunni scholarly prowess in Ayyubid Egypt, while his posthumous reputation for sanctity developed in conjunction with the cult of Sayyida Nafisa, which first flourished under the Ayyubids' predecessors, the Isma'ili Fatimids.

VENERATION AND BUILDING

At his death in 204/820, Shafi'i was interred in Ibn 'Abd al-Hakam's family plot. Today, Shafi'i's grand domed mausoleum with attached mosque stands at the geographic and symbolic center of Cairo's sprawling Southern Cemetery, known as the Lesser Qarafa; its main avenue is called Imam Shafi'i Street. The story of how it got there is one of patronage and power, both secular and spiritual. The tomb complex has been at the center of architectural innovation, schemes to consolidate political authority, and religious controversies about building commemorative structures over graves.

It is unclear when the first structure surrounding Shafi'i's tomb was built, but it probably predates the Fatimids, an Isma'ili Shi'i dynasty that ruled Egypt from 358/969 to 557/1171. The Fatimids built mausoleum shrines for a number of male and, notably, female 'Alid figures. The Sunni Ayyubids who overthrew the Fatimids adapted the latter's building practices to promote their own religio-political agendas. Caroline Williams suggests that the Ayyubids, "in a triumphant assertion of their own orthodox rule, built in the midst of the 'Alid tombs the largest single-domed mausoleum in the Qarafa, a shrine to a great Sunni teacher and saint, Imam Shafi'i, which was architecturally, decoratively, and functionally a successor to the Fatimid mausolea" (1985, 57).

The Ayyubids also borrowed from Syrian or Persian influences by linking a *madrasa*, a college devoted to the religious sciences, with a tomb. The college dedicated to Shafi'i was the first such example in Egypt, and in fact predated his mausoleum. It was commissioned by the sultan Salah al-Din, better known as Saladin.

Saladin was a partisan of Shafi'ism – in Aleppo he had championed it over the previous ruler's preference for Hanafism. The numerous colleges he established in Egypt thus had a dual function: to efface any vestiges of Fatimid rule and to promote the Shafi'i school over its Sunni counterparts. The construction, four years in the works, was completed in 576/1180. Shafi'i law, theology, and exegesis were taught. The first holder of the college's main chair, and apparent cheerleader for its establishment, was a Shafi'i scholar named al-Khushshani (d. 587/1191). Ibn Khallikan reports that he was buried under a dome at the foot of Shafi'i's grave with a grating separating the tombs; he does not seem to be there any longer. Perhaps he was moved when the mausoleum was built around the tomb two decades later, in 607–8/1211, by Saladin's nephew al-Malik al-Kamil. To make space for the mausoleum, numerous remains in the Banu Zahra cemetery were moved to another graveyard, though the tomb of Abdallah ibn 'Abd al-Hakam remains.

In building mausolea, sultans sought worldly prestige but also spiritual reward from association with sacred places and saintly figures. Al-Malik al-Kamil was no exception. He intended Shafi'i's mausoleum as a burial place for his mother, the Princess 'Adiliyya. Al-Kamil later tried (unsuccessfully) to get the mystic and poet Ibn al-Farid (d. 632/1235) to agree to be buried there. The sultan also used the site for more tangible patronage, bringing Qur'an reciters there and distributing water from it.

Other leaders over the centuries also used Shafi'i's complex to distribute charity. Mamluk sultans on the brink of warfare visited Shafi'i's mausoleum and gave alms to the needy. Al-Zahir Barquq did so before a confrontation with Tamerlane in 796/1394; Qansuh al-Ghawri (r. 906–22/1501–16), who is said to have added to the renovations of Shafi'i's mausoleum, made a similar visit, also providing alms before setting out on his ill-fated expedition against the Ottomans in 922/1516. A few years later, during a plague outbreak, his Ottoman successor used Shafi'i's shrine along with two others as a place to serve food to the populace.

Image 3 This sixteenth-century Ottoman history depicts the eponyms of the four Sunni legal schools. Clockwise from bottom right, they are Imam Malik, Imam Ahmad ibn Hanbal, Imam Shafi'i, and Abu Hanifa, identified here as "the Great Imam." Image courtesy of Topkapi Sarayi Museum.

Shafi'i's mausoleum continued to attract rulers' patronage in the Ottoman and post-Ottoman eras. The complex has been renovated and expanded several times. The distinctive cubical dome has been replaced at least twice. In the ninth/fifteenth century, the Mamluk sultan Qaytbay replaced the dome with a fancier one and added marble panels. The current dome was built in 1772 by the Ottoman governor 'Ali Bey al-Kabir not long after Khayr al-Din al-Ramli's fateful nap. Other internal decoration likewise dates from the eighteenth century. In 1892 a green fabric turban replaced a marble column as the marker for the location of Shafi'i's head; the impressive carved column remains, however, outside the tomb's enclosure.

Long before nineteenth-century European scholars and functionaries admired the tomb and its decorations (Frenchman H. de Vaujany, who had to obtain special permission to enter "la chapelle de l'imam," wrote that the cupola's "blue and red designs, circled by a sort of gilded wirework, have a charming effect"), Muslim travelers also marveled at it. Medieval guidebooks to Islamic Cairo list Shafi'i's mausoleum as a must-see. Famed travelogue writers Ibn Jubayr (d. 614/1217) and Ibn Battuta (d. 770/1368–9) praised its impressive scale, "admirable workmanship and marvelous construction, an exceedingly fine piece of architecture and exceptionally lofty" (Netton 1993, 279–80). Ibn Jubayr calls it "a shrine superb in beauty and size" (Netton 1993, 282). Today, Cairo has encroached on the madrasa, mosque, and mausoleum; it is difficult to appreciate the complex's original architectural impact.

FROM SHAYKH TO SAINT

Shafi'i is not the only jurist to have had a tomb erected in his honor become a draw for pious visitors. According to some stories, Shafi'i himself visited the tomb of Abu Hanifa frequently while he was in Baghdad. Ibn Hanbal is likewise buried in Baghdad, in the Harbiya quarter. His tomb, which Ibn Khallikan calls well-known and frequently visited by the pious, has suffered the ravages of time – after it was destroyed by the flooding of the Tigris in the seventh/thirteenth century, veneration shifted to the grave of his son 'Abdallah, buried in another cemetery. Malik ibn Anas was buried in the prestigious Medinan cemetery Jannat al-Baqi. The Saudi regime has since demolished the mausolea in that graveyard, including the structure that marked his burial place.

Despite the fact that tomb-building for prominent figures has obviously been common, debates about construction at grave sites began early and have persisted through Muslim history. For the most part such building has been tolerated, especially when tombs are on private land; a zealous minority has advocated and sometimes practiced demolition. There have also been acrimonious disputes about acceptable behavior at tombs. Shafi'i's mausoleum itself bears witness to debates over the boundaries of religiously correct practice: a green sticker pasted on his tomb enclosure, presumably by a pious visitor, attests to "The permissibility of seeking blessing by means of the Prophet's relics." The authority whose benediction is invoked for this practice is Ibn Hanbal, who reportedly used three of the Prophet's hairs over the course of his life and was buried with them. The appeal to Ibn Hanbal, whose reputation for sincere piety is uncontested, presumably seeks to allay fears of those who — despite the fact that they are visiting a saint's shrine — harbor doubts about potentially dubious practices.

Controversies are not confined to the shrine site. A YouTube video aimed at a somewhat broader audience shows a bearded and beturbaned scholar lecturing for two and a half minutes in impeccable Arabic about the permissibility of visiting the graves of the Prophet and the "friends [of God]." His justification, for which he quotes from al-Khatib al-Baghdadi's *History*, is that Shafi'i visited Abu Hanifa's grave daily. How, he asks, can one say that visiting the Prophet's grave and the graves of God's friends to seek blessing and ask their intercession (*tawassul*) is polytheism (*shirk*)? "Are they accusing Shafi'i of polytheism?" His culminating flourish depends on his audience's confidence in Shafi'i's orthodoxy: "And if Shafi'i is a polytheist according to them, then who is a Muslim?" (Wisely, the poster disabled comments for the video, which had been watched over 8,000 times when I saw it.)

Shafi'i's views play into other controversies over Sufism, another flashpoint in the current brouhaha over what constitutes acceptable Muslim belief and practice. He was not formally affiliated with any Sufi order, though he declares the compatibility of jurisprudence with mystical observance in one of his poems. He writes, "A jurist and a Sufi: do not only one be" (*Diwan* 34). Shafi'i's views on Sufism form part of online polemics between "traditionalists" and "Salafis" on websites such as livingislam.org. One particularly salient feature of G.F. Haddad's 1997 essay there, on "The Tasawwuf [or Sufism] of Shafi'i," is the way it invokes traditional texts in a new format: Ibn al-Jawzi's *Talbis Iblis*, which represents Shafi'i as disparaging Sufis, is cited by contemporary Salafis as evidence against Sufism; Haddad quotes other classical scholars to show that Ibn al-Jawzi "was not reliable when it came to reporting narrations." What is noteworthy is that Shafi'i is cited as an authority by all parties: Ibn al-Jawzi, contemporary Salafis, and neo-traditionalists. In Haddad's pious biographical notice for Shafi'i, found on the same site, he opines: "Shafi'i's attitude toward *tasawwuf* [Sufism] was as strict as with *kalam* [theology], and he both praised it and denigrated its abuse at the hands of its corrupters."

Can we know anything about his actual views on specific Sufi practices? We do know that he saw in revelation, especially prophetic sunna as transmitted via hadith, and in jurisprudence, the most important flowering of religion. His *Diwan* (88) speaks of particular "sciences" (*'ulum*, sing. *'ilm*) or areas of knowledge, with particular attention to jurisprudence and hadith:

> All sciences besides the Qur'an are busywork
> Except for hadith and the science of religious jurisprudence
>
> Knowledge is what follows "He related to us" (*haddathana*)
> And all besides that is the whisperings of Satan

Shafi'i's status as a "friend of God" is clearly posthumous. To the extent he achieved renown in his lifetime it was for his sharp mind, his skill in debate, and his redoubtable eloquence. But he would have been out of the mainstream of Muslim observance of the time if he did not consider some individuals to be particularly worthy of emulating, or to have particular spiritual merit that might induce one to spend time in their company in the hopes that some of the blessing might spill over onto oneself. One such figure is Sayyida Nafisa (d. 208/824).

In the vestibule between Shafi'i's mausoleum and its attached mosque hangs a genealogical chart showing the descendants of 'Ali, among them Nafisa, the great-granddaughter of 'Ali and Fatima's son Hasan. She was also the daughter-in-law of Ja'far al-Sadiq, an important Shi'i Imam. Her combination of impeccable lineage and reputation for renunciation made her a source of blessing as well as knowledge. The bare bones of her standard biography emerged more than a century after her death, according to Yusuf Raghib (1976); major embellishment, including her linkage with Shafi'i, seems to have begun around the same time her shrine cult emerged in the Fatimid period. Her biographers drew on Shafi'i's renown to buttress her scholarly reputation but most persistent have been the overtones of spiritual mentorship. The Western observer Joseph McPherson, relying on his own observations in twentieth-century Egypt, refers to it as "a kind of spiritual romance" (1941, 298), making the analogy to St. Francis and St. Claire. An essay in the quarterly publication of the neo-traditionalist American Zaytuna Institute makes explicit Shafi'i's recognition of her scholarly and spiritual authority: "Sayyidah Nafisah also possessed knowledge that was eagerly sought by the greatest scholars of her time, who made frequent visits to her... Her most illustrious visitor was undoubtedly Imam Shafi'i, by consensus the most knowledgeable man on earth at that time. He often asked for her prayers ..." Later, when her response to his request for prayers makes it clear that he will soon die, he requests that she participate in his funeral (Badawi 2007).

Shifting accounts of this funeral, and Nafisa's participation in it, can shed light on several interlinked issues, including saintliness, social power, and the shifting concerns of the biographical tradition.

Numerous accounts — again, in her biographies rather than his — inform us that Nafisa prayed over Shafi'i. Most accounts suggest that she participated from inside her home, or from the nearby mosque. But stories change to suit new contexts. Some recent accounts imply or declare outright that Nafisa led other mourners in the collective funeral prayer. Funerals thus remain an important site for the construction of social meaning. The twenty-first-century narratives in which Nafisa leads the prayer aim to prove a point about Muslim religious authority, clearly speaking to the controversy over female leadership of public and mixed-gender prayer. Premodern accounts care little for this and are instead concerned with attesting to Shafi'i's recognition of Nafisa's spiritual merit — hence, his request that she pray over him and the carrying of his bier to her home en route to his burial place.

It is surprisingly difficult to get facts about Shafi'i's funeral, including who led it, though we can be fairly certain Nafisa did not enjoy that honor. Buwayti is sometimes said to have done so. The historian Mas'udi (d. 345/956) reports that the governor, al-Sari ibn al-Hakam, led the prayer; this is probable given that Shafi'i was on good terms with him and had at least some prominence. The lack of information on Shafi'i's funeral in even the hagiographic sources dedicated to him, in contradistinction to the way that the funeral of Ibn Hanbal is discussed, provides further evidence that Shafi'i's connection with sanctity emerged only slowly.

HAGIOGRAPHY

The veneration of Shafi'i as a saintly figure involves both physical and literary construction. The best example of this is the fifth/eleventh-century jurist Bayhaqi's massive biographical endeavor, *Shafi'i's Virtues*. It contains both "pious legends" and a great deal of purportedly factual information on mundane if not insignificant elements of Shafi'i's life. Jaques points out that Bayhaqi's retelling of Shafi'i's life resonates with, even "mimics" the narrative of the Prophet's life: "Shafi'i is described as a member of the Quraysh tribe and the Prophet's clan; his father dies when he is young" — I would add that he grew up poor and spent time with the Bedouin — "he travels to Mecca and Medina, as well as to other locales, looking for understandings and approaches to knowing God's will; and, ultimately, he is placed at the center of a group of devoted acolytes who, following his death, carried forward his ideas and legal theories" (2007, 159). Abu Zahra similarly echoes the prophetic model when he refers to Shafi'i as "a poor orphan from a noble lineage" (1948, 17).

Despite the fact that it would add to this vision of Shafi'i as prophet-like, the role of Mecca in Shafi'i's life is downplayed by his later biographers. Instead, anecdotes favor Iraqi, Egyptian, or even Yemeni locales for vital events in his lifetime. His travels between these locations are primary; what I believe to have been more time spent in Mecca than is usually acknowledged is glossed over, though the hadith scholar al-Nasa'i (d. 303/915), known best for his hadith compilation, treats Shafi'i and his students (regardless of their geographic location) as jurisprudentially Meccan. The prominence of Iraq and especially Egypt in later accounts of his life can be chalked up to the crucial role of his disciples from these locales in their later influence. A story attributed to Ibn 'Abd al-Hakam asserts a peculiarly Egyptian authority for Shafi'i, enhancing the prestige of that branch of the school that ultimately sprang up around him. Shafi'i's pregnant mother had a dream:

> It was as if Jupiter came forth from her womb and descended in Egypt, but a sliver of its rays reached every land. The interpreters of dreams explained that a learned man would come forth from her whose learning would be for Egypt's people alone, but then it would spread into the remaining lands.
>
> (IK 22)

In addition to enhancing Egypt's prestige, the miraculous nature of this maternal vision links the mundane world of teaching circles and juridical treatises directly to the numinous.

CONCLUSION

Shafi'i's *Risala* is the kind of text for which words like outdated were invented. Modern scholars writing about Shafi'i's theory use terms like basic and crude, though some also add "ingenious" or "brilliant." One deems his terminology "rudimentary" but his theory "sophisticated." (A less flattering view says "rudimentary" and "erratic.") People read the *Risala* for historical interest, not as a primer for legal method. Its organization and terminology perplex later scholars; it represents a detour from legal theory's ultimate path. Yet its central preoccupation, how to interpret divine guidance, remains vital. Far from being dry legal history, the question of how Qur'an and sunna relate to one another is a live issue. Modern discussions tend to blindness about the past; Shafi'i's accomplishment in situating prophetic tradition in the form of hadith squarely within both revelation and law has had undeniably profound effects for the Sunni tradition as a whole and therefore must be engaged, if only better to understand today's debates.

The focus on hadith recurs throughout Shafi'i's corpus and provides the best entry point to his work for those who wish to engage his ideas. The question of hadith has renewed importance in modernity. Aisha Musa's recent translation of the *Summation of Knowledge* is set within a monograph titled *Hadith as Scripture*. The twin claims of Musa's historical argument are unimpeachable: the acceptance of hadith as a second source of scripture alongside the Qur'an was not a foregone conclusion and Shafi'i's role in making it so was significant. But her title carries an unspoken question mark. She frames her presentation of Shafi'i to highlight the negative elements of the victory Shafi'i won for hadith.

Musa is far from alone in questioning the place of hadith as a source of norms alongside the Qur'an. In the twentieth century, hadith came under sharp criticism from reformists of various stripes, especially in South Asia, whose rejection of hadith has:

> had a major influence as a catalyst, sparking controversy and setting the agenda for modern discussions of Prophetic authority. The issues raised by these deniers of hadith – the nature of revelation, the scope of prophetic authority, the reliability of tradition literature [i.e. hadith] – have been the main concerns in the modern crisis of religious authority ...
>
> (Brown 1999, 42)

Other widespread transformations – in literacy, education, print, the Internet – have also dramatically reshaped ideas about who is qualified to address religious questions and on what basis. Paradoxically, Shafi'i's accomplishment in insisting that revelation rather than authoritative pronouncements of scholars was the sole determinant of legitimate guidance has fed into this dynamic. However, although he did not consider the positions of scholars dispositive on their own, he certainly considered experts necessary for assessing and interpreting scriptural texts, especially hadith.

In Shafi'i's time, certain kinds of knowledge were simply not available to everyone. He would have been shocked to discover hadith collections for use without specialist guidance. And in translation! Reports are quoted without their chains of transmission and keyword-searchable online databases substitute for expert knowledge. A few modern scholars have insisted on the ability independently to verify chains of transmission, but many Muslims cite only the canonical compiler, usually Bukhari or Muslim. Although he would be scandalized by many of its elements, in some ways the current situation is an outgrowth of Shafi'i's concern with delimiting a finite body of revealed texts on which interpreters can operate. It is no accident that the compilers of the six canonical Sunni hadith collections in the century after his death were Shafi'is. Nor is it accidental that written (now digital) canons became central. As El Shamsy argues: "Canonization and writing thus constitute a mutually generating complex in the history of early Islamic law: the former endows the revelatory sources with authority and meaning, and the latter encases them in a stable form that lends itself to systematic analysis" (2009, 279). In other words, when it comes not to collection but to canonization, Shafi'i started it.

The Muslim world in the twentieth and twenty-first centuries is undergoing a process in some respects parallel to that which confronted Shafi'i in Egypt in the early ninth century. Questions about interpretive authority and the role and function of texts and their interpreters are vital. His answers to fundamental queries about language and law cannot be applied directly to the twenty-first century but his basic preoccupations remain relevant. The issues he grappled with were major ones. He sweated the small stuff, preoccupied with fine points of ritual observance and legal precepts, but maintained the connection between quotidian details and the big picture, a picture in which God's comprehensive revelation means that no matter is left unregulated.

Connecting the small details with the bigger picture is also an essential part of writing a biography. A biographer must feel that her subject has importance beyond his or her individual life, otherwise there is no point to the exercise. This volume has introduced the life and thought of one of Islam's foundational figures. I have tried, briefly, to situate Shafi'i within his historical and intellectual context. He was very much a man of his time and place — or rather, given his incessant wanderings, places. But he also accomplished things that had a lasting impact on Islamic history. Shafi'i's reputation as the founder or "father and mother" of Islamic jurisprudence is an attempt to personalize a much larger process. Shifting images of Shafi'i as master architect and master compromiser, the renewer of his age, speak to our need to make sense of his life, not only his actual significance. The processes through which major tendencies and overlapping circles of influence coalesced into four discrete schools named for long-dead "founders" owe much to shifting regional and political dynamics but also to chance: some men had longer lives than others, taught more students, had more books circulated. Shafi'i's status today is partially a result of the work he did and partially a result of the deeds attributed to him, rightly or wrongly, by his disciples and their intellectual descendants. Even if we shun the exaggerated claims of his achievements and merits that both medieval hagiographers and some modern commentators have espoused, adopting a more realistic picture of his accomplishments, we are still left with a man whose place in Muslim history is undeniable.

A tradition – perhaps invented and certainly circulated by Shafi'i's followers – states that each century, a renewer will appear to set things to rights among Muslims. 'Umar ibn 'Abd al-'Aziz, an Umayyad caliph whose piety and competence often get him listed alongside the first four "rightly guided" caliphs (including in a statement attributed to Shafi'i) was the first such renewer; Shafi'i, the second. The construction of Shafi'i as prophet-like, as renewer of the faith, as founder of Islamic law, and as a saintly intercessor who can cure illnesses and redress grievances happens among scholars of the Shafi'i legal school and ordinary Muslims, Egyptians and non-Egyptians. His enduring significance is both deeper and broader than his undeniable contribution to the science of jurisprudence and the formation of the core of the Sunni intellectual tradition. A lecturer in fashion design from Egypt's Helwan University, whom I met by chance in Washington DC while writing this book, was delighted to talk about this paragon. She told me, "Imam Shafi'i is one of my favorite people in the world."

FURTHER READING

Full citations for works listed here are found in the bibliography.

Few of Shafi'i's numerous biographers have written in English. Two good short biographies are Lowry (2005), which focuses on his works, and Chaumont's entry in the second edition of the *Encyclopaedia of Islam*. The Arabic biography by the Egyptian jurist Muhammad Abu Zahra (d. 1974) (Abu Zahra 1948) has been abridged, translated, and published with his biographies of the other Sunni eponyms (Abu Zahrah 2001). Those who read Arabic ought also to consult the interpretive study by Nasr Hamid Abu Zayd (d. 2010) (Abu Zayd 2007); a précis of one chapter has been translated into French (Abou Zeid 1999). A biography by the late Indonesian scholar 'Abd al-Salam (1988) draws extensively from the premodern Arabic sources. Of these, I have relied most on works by Ibn Abi Hatim al-Razi and Bayhaqi, supplemented by standard biographical dictionaries. Most resist non-specialist exploration, with their peculiar organizing principles and stylistic conventions. One exception gets around the language barrier, though not the genre norms: Ibn Khallikan's biographical dictionary was translated into English in the nineteenth century; it was recently reprinted (Ibn Khallikan 2010) but the full text of the original can be found online in the public domain.

A few of Shafi'i's methodological writings are available in translation. Khadduri's rendering of the *Risala* (Shafi'i 1987) is sometimes clunky and his reordering of the text in some places is misleading, but it remains accessible. Semaan (1961) offers an overview, now dated, of the main ideas of the *Risala*, as well as a translation of the sections on abrogation. Lowry, whose specialist monograph (2007) on the *Risala* includes numerous newly translated excerpts, is preparing a full translation (Shafi'i forthcoming). In the meantime, he has translated selections from the *Disagreements between Hadith* with a brief introduction (Lowry forthcoming). Musa's translation of the *Summation of Knowledge* (Musa 2008) also includes a good introduction to the text and its context as well as interesting exploration of parallel contemporary debates.

Like his collected poems, published in several widely available editions, Shafi'i's writings on positive law ('Abd al-Muttalib [Shafi'i 2001] is best) remain untranslated. Works belonging to his contemporaries can help give a sense of the scope and range of ideas with which Shafi'i was conversant. There are several English versions of Malik's *Muwatta'*, though as yet no satisfactory scholarly translation. Spectorsky (1993) has translated Ibn Hanbal's responsa, along with some by Ishaq ibn Rahawayh, on marriage and divorce with a very useful introduction. The *Muwatta' Shaybani* is available in English with parallel Arabic (Shaybani 2004). Khadduri has also translated Shaybani's writings on war and international relations (Shaybani 1966).

For early Islamic legal history, Hallaq (2005) is likely to replace Schacht (1967) as the standard introduction. Schacht's scholarship on Shafi'i remains important, though monographs and articles by Lowry (various), Melchert (various), Brockopp (various), and Dutton (various), among others, have modified some of his conclusions. The most recent contributions to the literature are Yahia (2009) and El Shamsy (2009). All of these contain bibliographies pointing to further studies.

Kennedy (2005) and Bennison (2009) provide highly readable histories of the Abbasid caliphate. Hodgson (1974) remains unsurpassed as an overview of the high culture of the central lands of Islam; for the early legal tradition, see volume 1, *The Classical Age of Islam*. On saint veneration and tomb visitation in Egypt, as well as the fourteenth-century controversies over it, consult Taylor (1999).

Readers wanting to sample primary sources can dip into the thirty-eight-volume English translation of Tabari's *History of Prophets and Kings* (Tabari, various); volumes 29–32 span the period of Shafi'i's life. (Alternatively, Tabari 1988 covers from before Shafi'i's birth to 193/809, the year of Harun al-Rashid's death.) Those seeking anecdotes about Shafi'i will be disappointed, though. A glance through the index shows that Abu Hanifa appears in four volumes, his disciples Abu Yusuf and Shaybani, like Ibn Hanbal, in two apiece, and the long-lived Malik in six, with at least eight separate mentions in one volume alone. Curiously, Tabari, an independent jurist who trained with Shafi'i's disciple Rabi', makes no mention of Shafi'i at all.

BIBLIOGRAPHY

In alphabetizing entries, I have ignored the Arabic article "al" as well as the letter 'ayn.

LIST OF ABBREVIATIONS USED IN THE TEXT

B – Bayhaqi
IAH – Ibn Abi Hatim al-Razi
IK – Ibn Khallikan

Diwan – unless otherwise noted, citations to 1971 edition and translations mine
Umm – citations to 1993 edition and translations mine
Risala – unless otherwise noted, citations to 1987 trans. Khadduri, often modified
Summation – in Musa 2008, trans. Musa
Q. – Qur'an – unless otherwise noted, translations mine

SHAFI'I'S WRITINGS IN ARABIC AND TRANSLATION

al-Shāfi'ī, Muḥammad ibn Idrīs. 1940. *Al-Risāla fi uṣūl al-fiqh*, ed. Aḥmad Muḥammad Shākir. Cairo: al-Ḥalabī
———. 1940. *Jimā' al-'Ilm* (*The Summation [or Amalgamation] of Knowledge*), ed. Aḥmad Muḥammad Shākir. Cairo: Maṭba'at al-Ma'ārif, 1940. Trans. Aisha Musa, in Musa (2008)
———. 1971. *Dīwān al-Shāfi'ī*, ed. Muḥammad 'Afīf al-Zu'bī. Beirut: Dār al-Nūr

———. 1985. *Ikhtilāf al-Ḥadīth (bi riwāyat al-Rabīʿ ibn Sulaymān al-Murādī) (Disagreements between Hadith — according to the narration of al-Rabiʿ)*, ed. ʿĀmir Aḥmad Ḥaydar. Beirut: Muʾassasat al-Kutub al-Thaqāfīya. Partial translation in Lowry (forthcoming)

———. 1987. *Al-Shāfiʿī's Risāla: Treatise on the Foundations of Islamic Jurisprudence*, trans. Majid Khadduri, 2nd edn. Cambridge: Islamic Texts Society

———. 1993. *Al-Umm*. ed. 9 vols. Beirut: Dār al-Kutub al-ʿIlmīya. Contains shorter treatises along with an edition of Muzanī's *Mukhtaṣar*

———. 2001. *Al-Umm*. ed. Rifʿat Fawzī ʿAbd al-Muṭṭalib, 11 vols, al-Manṣūra, Egypt: Dār al-Wafāʾ. Contains an edition of the *Risāla* along with shorter treatises

———. forthcoming. *Al-Risāla*. trans. Joseph E. Lowry. New York and Abu Dhabi: New York University Press, Abu Dhabi Library of Arabic Literature

ARABIC BIOGRAPHICAL, HISTORICAL, AND LEGAL SOURCES

ʿAbd al-Salām, Aḥmad Nahrāwī. 1988. *Al-Imām al-Shāfiʿī fī madhhabayhi al-qadīm wa-al-jadīd: ḥayātuhu wa-ʿaṣruh, uṣūluhu wa-fiqhuh, aṣḥābuhu wa-anṣāruhu fī nashr madhhabih, athāruhu al-ʿilmīya wa-kutubuh (Imam Shafiʿi and His Old and New Doctrines: his life and his times, his sources and his jurisprudence, his companions and those who helped spread his doctrines, his scholarly impact and his books)*. [Cairo]: A.N. ʿAbd al-Salām

Abū Zahra, Muḥammad. [1948]. *Al-Shāfiʿī: ḥayātuhu wa-ʿaṣruhu — ārāʾuhu wa-fiqhuhu (Al-Shāfiʿī: His life and his times — his views and his jurisprudence)*. 2nd edn. [Cairo]: Dār al-Fikr al-ʿArabī

Abū Zayd, Naṣr Ḥāmid. 2007. *Al-Imām al-Shāfiʿī wa-taʾsīs al-īdiyūlūjīya al-wasaṭīya (Imam Shafiʿi and the Foundation of Moderate Ideology)*. al-Dār al-Bayḍāʾ: al-Markaz al-Thaqāfī al-ʿArabī

Bayhaqī, Aḥmad ibn al-Ḥusayn. 1971. *Manāqib al-Shāfiʿī (Shafiʿi's Virtues)*, 2 vols, ed. al-Sayyid Aḥmad Ṣaqr. Cairo: Maktabat Dār al-Turāth

Ibn Abī Ḥātim al-Rāzī. 1953. *Adab al-Shāfiʿī wa manāqibuhu* (*Shafiʿi's Manners and Virtues*), ed. ʿAbd al-Ghani ʿAbd al-Khāliq. Beirut: Dār al-Kutub al-ʿIlmīya

Ibn Ḥajar al-ʿAsqalānī. 1994. *Tahdhīb al-tahdhīb* (*The Refinement of the Refinement*), ed. Muṣṭafā ʿAbd al-Qādir ʿAṭā. Beirut: Dār al-Kutub al-ʿIlmīya

Ibn Khallikan. 1998. *Wafayāt al-aʿyān wa anbāʾ abnāʾ al-zamān* (*Deaths of Notables and News of the Children of the Times*), eds Yūsuf ʿAlī Ṭawīl and Maryam Qāsim Ṭawīl. Beirut: Dār al-Kutub al-ʿIlmīya. Trans. William MacGuckin de Slane, as *Ibn Khallikan's Biographical Dictionary*, 4 vols. New York: Cosimo Classics, 2010 (I have consulted this translation but usually provide my own slightly more literal rendering of the Arabic)

Ibn Qāḍī Shubha. 2003. *Kitāb Manāqib al-Imām al-Shāfiʿī wa Ṭabaqāt Aṣḥābihi min Tarīkh al-Islām liʾ l-Ḥāfiẓ Abī ʿAbdallāh al-Dhahabī* (*Book of Imam Shafiʿi's Virtues and Biographies of his Companions from Dhahabī's History of Islam*), ed. ʿAbd al-ʾAzīz Fayyaḍ Marfūsh. Damascus: Dar al-Bashāʾir

Mālik ibn Anas. 1989. *Al-Muwaṭṭaʾ liʾ l-Imām Mālik ibn Anas, bi riwāyat Yaḥyā ibn Yaḥyā ibn Kathīr al-Laythī al-Andalūsī* (*The Muwaṭṭaʾ of Imam Malik ibn Anas, transmitted by Yahya ibn Yahya ibn Kathīr al-Laythī al-Andalūsī*). Beirut: Dār al-Fikr

al-Qadi, Wadad. 1989. "Riḥlat al-Shāfiʿī ilā ʾl-Yaman" ("Shafiʿi's Journey to Yemen"), in *Arabian Studies in Honour of Mahmoud Ghul: Symposium at Yarmouk University, 8–11 December 1984*. Wiesbaden: Otto Harrassowitz, pp. 127–141

[Saḥnūn b. Saʿīd al-Tanūkhī] Mālik b. Anas. 1323 AH [1905–1906]. *Al-Mudawwana al-Kubrā* (*The Major Compendium*). Beirut: Dār Ṣādir

al-Shaybānī, Muḥammad. 1965. *Kitāb al-Ḥujja ʿala ahl al-Madīna* (*Book of Refutation of the People of Medina*). Hyderabad: Lajnat Iḥyāʾ al-Maʿārif al-Nuʿmānīya

———. 1966. *The Islamic Law of Nations: Shaybani's Siyar*, trans. Majid Khadduri. Baltimore, MD: Johns Hopkins University Press

———. 1997. *Muwaṭṭaʾ to al-Imam Mālik, bi riwāyat Muḥammad ibn al-Ḥasan al-Shaybānī*. Beirut: Al-Maṭbaʿa al-ʿIlmīya. Trans. *The Muwatta of Imam Muhammad*, trans. Mohammed Abdurrahman, Abdassamad Clarke, and Asadullah Yate. London: Turath Publishing, 2004

al-Subkī, Tāj al-Dīn. 1999. *Ṭabaqāt al-Shāfiʿīya al-kubrā* (*Major Biographical Dictionary of the Shafiʿis*), ed. Muṣṭafā ʿAbd al-Qādir Aḥmad ʿAṭā. Beirut: Dār al-Kutub al-ʿIlmīya

ʿUways, Sayyid. 1978. *Rasāʾil ilā ʾl-Imām al-Shāfiʿī: ẓahirat irsāl al-rasāʾil ilā ḍarīḥ al-Imām al-Shāfiʿī* (*Letters sent to the Tomb of Imam Shafiʿi*). Cairo: Dār al-Shāyiʿ li ʾl-Nashr

WORKS IN EUROPEAN LANGUAGES

Abou Zeid, Nasr [Abū Zayd, Naṣr Ḥāmid]. 1999. "Sunna et Coran dans la pensée de Shâfiʾî," in *Critique du discourse religieux*, trans. Mohamad Chairet. Arles: Sindbad-Actes Sud, pp. 93–125

Abū Zahrah, Muḥammad. 2001. *The Four Imams: Their Lives and Teachings of their Founders: Imam ash-Shafiʿi (150/767–204/820)*, trans. Aisha Bewley. London: Dar al-Taqwa

Adly, Emad. 2008. "The Saint, the Sheikh, and the Adulteress: Letters from the Heart Addressed to Imam al-Shafiʿi in Cairo," in Baudouin Dupret, Barbara Drieskens and Annelies Moors, eds, *Narratives of Truth in Islamic Law*. London: I.B. Tauris, pp. 123–139

Ahsan, M.M. 1979. *Social Life under the ʿAbbasids*. London and New York: Longman

Algar, Hamid. 2002. *Wahhabism: A Critical Essay*. Oneonta, NY: Islamic Publications International

Ansari, Zafar Ishaq. 1994. "The Significance of Shāfiʿī's Criticism of the Medinese School of Law," in *Islamic Studies, Occasional Papers* 5. Islamabad: Islamic Research Institute

al-ʿAydarūs, ʿAbd al-Qādir. 2001. "The Autobiography of al-ʿAydarūs," in Dwight Reynolds, ed., *Interpreting the Self: Autobiography in the Arabic Literary Tradition*. Berkeley: University of California Press, pp. 208–215

al-Badawi, Mostafa. 2007. "Nafisah the Ascentic," *Seasons* (The Zaytuna Institute, California) 4(1)

Bedir, Murteza. 2002. "An Early Response to Shāfiʿī: ʿĪsā b. Abān on the Prophetic Report (*Khabar*)," *Islamic Law and Society* 9(3): 285–311

Bennison, Amira K. 2009. *The Great Caliphs*. New Haven, CT: Yale University Press

Bernards, Monique and Nawas, John. 2003. "The Geographic Distribution of Muslim Jurists during the First Four Centuries AH," *Islamic Law and Society* 10(2): 161–181

Brockopp, Jonathan E. 1998. "Early Islamic Jurisprudence in Egypt: Two Scholars and Their *Mukhtaṣars*," *International Journal of Middle East Studies* 30: 167–182

———. 2000. *Early Mālikī Law: Ibn 'Abd al-Ḥakam and his Major Compendium of Jurisprudence*. Leiden: Brill

Brown, Daniel. 1999. *Rethinking Tradition in Modern Islamic Thought*. Cambridge: Cambridge University Press

Burton, John. 1990. *The Sources of Islamic Law: Islamic Theories of Abrogation*. Edinburgh: Edinburgh University Press

———. 2003. "Qur'ān and Sunnah: A Case of Cultural Disjunction," in Herbert Berg, ed., *Islamic History and Civilization* 49: *Method and Theory in the Study of Islamic Origins*. Leiden: Brill, pp. 137–157

Calder, Norman. 1983. "*Ikhtilâf* and *Ijmâ'* in Shâfi'î's Risâla," *Studia Islamica* 58: 55–81

———. 1993. *Studies in Early Muslim Jurisprudence*. Oxford: Clarendon Press

Chaumont, Éric. 2006. "al-Shāfi'ī" and "al-Shāfi'īya," in P. Bearman, Th. Bianquis, C.E. Bosworth, E. van Donzel and W.P. Heinrichs, eds, *Encyclopaedia of Islam*, 2nd edn. Leiden: Brill Online (print edition, vol. 9, pp. 181 ff.)

Coulson, Noel. 1964. *A History of Islamic Law*. Edinburgh: Edinburgh University Press

de Vaujany, H. Comte. 1883. *Le Caire et ses environs: caractères, moeurs, coutumes des Égyptiens modernes*. Paris: E. Plon.

Dodge, Bayard, ed. and trans. 1970. *The Fihrist of al-Nadim: A Tenth-century Survey of Muslim Culture*, vol. 1. New York: Columbia University Press

Dutton, Yasin. 2000. *The Origins of Islamic Law: The Qur'an, the Muwaṭṭa', and Madinan 'Amal*. Richmond, Surrey: Curzon Press

El Kadi, Galila and Bonnamy, Alain. 2007. *Architecture for the Dead: Cairo's Medieval Necropolis*. Cairo: American University in Cairo Press

El Shamsy, Ahmed. 2007. "The First Shāfi'ī: The Traditionalist Legal Thought of Abū Ya'qūb al-Buwayṭī," *Islamic Law and Society* 14(3): 301–341

———. 2009. "From Tradition to Law: The Origins and Early Development of the Shāfiʿī School of Law in Ninth-Century Egypt." Doctoral dissertation, Harvard University

———. Forthcoming. "Al-Shāfiʿī's Written Corpus: A Source-critical Study," *Journal of the American Oriental Society*

Graham, William A. 1993. "Traditionalism in Islam: An Essay in Interpretation," special issue "Religion and History," *Journal of Interdisciplinary History* 23(3): 495–522

———. 1997. *Divine Word and Prophetic Word in Early Islam: A Reconsideration of the Sources, with Special Reference to the Divine Saying or Ḥadîth Qudsî*. The Hague: Mouton

Haddad, G.F. 1997. "The Tasawwuf [or Sufism] of Shafi'i," 6 June. Available at: http://mac.abc.se/home/onesr/f/Tasawwuf of Al-Shafii.htm (accessed May 2011)

——— 2003. "Imam al-Shafi'i," 3 April. Available at: http://www.livingislam.org/n/shfi_e.html (accessed May 2011)

Hallaq, Wael B. 1993. "Was Al-Shafi'i the Master Architect of Islamic Jurisprudence?" *International Journal of Middle East Studies* 25(4): 587–605

———. 1997. *A History of Islamic Legal Theories*. Cambridge: Cambridge University Press

———. 2005. *The Origins and Evolution of Islamic Law*. Cambridge: Cambridge University Press

Harman, Claire. 2005. *Myself and the Other Fellow: A Life of Robert Louis Stevenson*. New York: HarperCollins

Heffening, W. 1913–36. "al-Shāfiʿī," in M.Th. Houtsma, T.W. Arnold, R. Basset, R. Hartmann, A.J. Wensinck, H.A.R. Gibb, W. Heffening, and E. Lévi-Provençal, eds, *Encyclopaedia of Islam*, vol. 2. Leiden: Brill, pp. 252–254

Hodgson, Marshall. 1974. *The Venture of Islam: Conscience and History in a World Civilization*, 3 vols. Chicago: University of Chicago Press

Hoffman-Ladd, Valerie J. 1992. "Devotion to the Prophet and His Family in Egyptian Sufism," *International Journal of Middle East Studies* 24(4): 615–637

Hurvitz, Nimrod. 2000. "Schools of Law and Historical Context: Re-examining the Formation of the Ḥanbalī *Madhhab*," *Islamic Law and Society* 7(1): 37–64

Jaques, R. Kevin. 2007. "The Other Rabīʿ: Biographical Traditions and the Development of Early Shāfiʿī Authority," *Islamic Law and Society* 14(2): 143–179

Kamali, Mohammad Hashim. 1991. *Principles of Islamic Jurisprudence*. Cambridge: Islamic Texts Society

Kennedy, Hugh. 2005. *When Baghdad Ruled the Muslim World: The Rise and Fall of Islam's Greatest Dynasty*. Cambridge, MA: Da Capo Press

Kern, Friedrich 1904. "Zwei Urkunden vom Imām aš-Šāfiʿī," *Mitteilungen des Seminars für Orientalische Sprachen* 7: 53–68

Lowry, Joseph E. 2002. "Does Shāfiʿī Have a Theory of 'Four Sources' of Law?" in Bernard G. Weiss, ed., *Studies in Islamic Legal Theory*. Leiden: Brill, pp. 23–50

———. 2004. "The Legal Hermeneutics of al-Shāfiʿī and Ibn Qutayba: A Reconsideration," *Islamic Law and Society* 11(1): 1–41

———. 2005. "Muhammad ibn Idris al-Shafiʿi," in Shawkat Toorawa and Michael Cooperson, eds, *Dictionary of Literary Biography*, vol. 311: *Arabic Literary Culture, 500–925*. Detroit: Thompson Gale, pp. 308–317

———. 2007. *Early Islamic Legal Theory: The Risāla of Muḥammad ibn Idrīs al-Shāfiʿī*. Leiden: Brill

———. 2008. "Some Preliminary Observations on al-Šāfiʿī and Later Uṣūl al-fiqh: The Case of the Term *bayān*," *Arabica* 55(5–6): 505–527

———. forthcoming. "Al-Shāfiʿī's Life and Thought and Selections from his *Ikhtilāf al-ḥadīth*," in O. Arabi, D. Powers and S. Spectorsky, eds, *Islamic Legal Thought: A Compendium of Muslim Jurists*. Leiden, Brill

McPherson, Joseph W. 1941. *The Moulids of Egypt (Egyptian Saints-days)*. Cairo: Ptd. N.M. Press

Makdisi, George. 1984. "The Juridical Theology of Shâfiʿî: Origins and Significance of *Uṣûl al-Fiqh*," *Studia Islamica* 59: 5–47

Melchert, Christopher. 1997. *The Formation of the Sunni Schools of Law, 9th–10th Centuries CE*. Studies in Islamic Law and Society, vol. 4. Leiden: Brill

———. 2001. "Traditionist-Jurisprudents and the Framing of Islamic Law," *Islamic Law and Society* 8(3): 383–406

———. 2003. "The Early History of Islamic Law," in Herbert Berg, ed., *Method and Theory in the Study of Islamic Origins*. Islamic History and Civilization 49. Leiden: Brill, pp. 293–324

———. 2004. "The Formation of the Sunni Schools of Law," in Wael B. Hallaq, ed., *The Formation of Islamic Law*. The Formation of the Classical Islamic World 27. Aldershot: Ashgate/Variorum, pp. 351–366

———. 2004. "The Meaning of *Qāla 'l-Shāfi'ī* in Ninth-century Sources," in James E. Montgomery, ed., *'Abbasid Studies*, occasional papers of the School of 'Abbasid Studies. Orientalia Lovaniensia Analecta 135. Leuven: Peeters, pp. 277–301

Musa, Aisha. 2008. *Ḥadīth as Scripture: Discussions on the Authority of Prophetic Traditions in Islam*. Houndmills: Palgrave Macmillan

Netton, Ian Richard. 1993. "Tourist *Adab* and Cairene Architecture: The Mediaeval Paradigm of Ibn Jubayr and Ibn Battutah," in Mustansir Mir with Jarl E. Fossum, eds, *The Literary Heritage of Classical Islam: Arabic and Islamic Studies in Honor of James A. Bellamy*. Princeton, NJ: The Darwin Press, pp. 275–284

Rāġib, Yūsuf. 1976. "Al-Sayyida Nafīsa, sa légende, son culte et son cimetière," *Studia Islamica* 44: 61–86

Rosenthal, Franz. 1997. "The Stranger in Medieval Islam," *Arabica* 44(1): 35–75

Schacht, Joseph. 1953. "On Shāfi'ī's Life and Personality," in *Studia Orientalia Ioanni Pedersen*. Einar Munksgaard: Hauniae, pp. 318–326

———. 1967. *The Origins of Muhammadan Jurisprudence*. Oxford: Clarendon Press

Schoeler, Gregor. 2006. *The Oral and the Written in Early Islam*, ed. James E. Montgomery, trans. Uwe Vagelpohl. New York: Routledge

Semaan, Khalil I. 1961. *Ash-Shāfi'ī's Risālah: Basic Ideas*. Lahore: Sh. Muhammad Ashraf

Shehaby, Nabil. 1982. "*'Illa* and *Qiyās* in Early Islamic Legal Theory," *Journal of the American Oriental Society* 102(1): 27–46

Spectorsky, Susan A., ed. and trans. 1993. *Chapters on Marriage and Divorce: Responses of Ibn Ḥanbal and Ibn Rāhwayh*. Austin: University of Texas Press

———. 2002. "Sunna in the Responses of Isḥāq b. Rāhwayh," in Bernard G. Weiss, ed., *Studies in Islamic Legal Theory*. Leiden: Brill, pp. 51–74

Stewart, Devin. 2002. "Muḥammad b. Dā'ūd al-Ẓāhirī's Manual of Jurisprudence, *al-Wuṣūl ilā ma'rifat al-uṣūl*," in Bernard G. Weiss, ed., *Studies in Islamic Legal Theory*. Leiden: Brill, pp. 99–158

al-Ṭabarī, Muḥammad ibn Jarīr. *The History of al-Ṭabarī* (various translators, various dates). Albany: SUNY Press
———. 1988. *The Early 'Abbasi Caliphate*, trans. John Alden Williams. Cambridge: Cambridge University Press
Taylor, Christopher S. 1999. *In the Vicinity of the Righteous: Ziyāra and the Veneration of Muslim Saints in Late Medieval Egypt*. Leiden: Brill
Tucker, Judith E. 2001. "Biography as History: The Exemplary Life of Khayr al-Din al-Ramli," in Mary Ann Fay, ed., *Auto/Biography and the Construction of Identity and Community in the Middle East*. New York: Palgrave, pp. 9–18
Vishanoff, David R. 2011. *The Formation of Islamic Hermeneutics: How Sunni Legal Theorists Imagined a Revealed Law*. American Oriental Series no. 93, ed. Stephanie W. Jamison. New Haven, CT: American Oriental Society
Williams, Caroline. 1985. "The cult of 'Alid saints in the Fatimid monuments of Cairo, Part II: The mausolea," *Muqarnas* 3: 39–60
Yahia, Mohyddin. 2009. *Šāfiʿī et les deux sources de la loi islamique*. Turnhout, Belgium: Brepols

INDEX

1001 Arabian Nights, The, 15

al-'Abbas ibn Musa, 32
Abbasids, 15–20, 32
'Abd al-Rahman ibn Mahdi, 48
'Abd Manaf, 2
'Abdallah (companion), 32
ablution, 66
abrogation, 61
Abu Bakr, 16, 17, 54
Abu Hanifa, 18, 20, 21, 22, 24–5, 29, 55, 56, 86, 89, 90, 91–2, 106, 107, 119
Abu Nuwas, 7
Abu Thawr, 30, 31, 36
Abu Yusuf Ya'qub, 21–2, 30, 44, 49, 86, 90, 119
Abu Zahra, Muhammad, 19, 27, 69, 74, 111, 117
Abu Zayd, Nasr Hamid, 77, 117
Abu Zur'a, 35
Abu Zurara al-Zuhri, 23
Abu'l-Hasan (Shafi'i's son), 40–1
Abu'l-Qasim 'Uthman ibn Sa'id al-Anmati, 94
accommodation costs, 45
'Adiliyya, Princess, 104
Adly, Emad, 101, 102
Ahsan, M. M., 45
al-Asma'i, 7
Algar, Hamid, 48
'Ali ibn Abi Talib, 4, 16, 17, 109
'Alid partisanship, 16–20, 103
'Amr ibn al-'As, 34
'Amr ibn 'Ubayd, 75
analogy, 28, 31, 36, 51, 52
Arabic language, 66–8
archery 4–7
al-Asamm, Abu Bakr, 73, 75
al-Asamm, Abu al-'Abbas, 56
al-Ash'ari, Abu'l-Hasan, 77, 95

Ash'arism, 77
Ashhab, 38
Ashkelon, 2
astronomy, 13, 14
al-Awza'i, 90
al-'Aydarus, 'Abd al-Qadir, 17
al-Azraqi, Muhammad ibn al-Walid 41
Ayyubids, 94, 103
al-Azhar, 95, 99

al-Badawi, Mostafa, 109
Baghdad, 5, 15, 19, 21, 27, 30–1, 32, 53, 94, 106
Bahrain, 95
baraka (blessing), 99
Basra, 45
bayan, 51, 58–61, 69, 72
al-Bayhaqi, Ahmad ibn Husayn, 24, 43, 56, 74, 83, 117; *Shafi'i's Virtues*, 110–11
Bedir, Murteza, 49
Bernards, Monique, 94
biographical dictionaries, xiv–xv, 21, 117
Brockopp, Jonathan, 32, 38, 118
Brown, Daniel, 114
al-Bukha, Isma'il, 11, 12, 55, 114
Bulbul (slave), 42
Buwayti, Abu Ya'qub, 35, 36–7, 80, 81, 93–4, 110

Calder, Norman, 49, 80
charity, 45–6
Chaumont, Éric, 20, 23, 32, 49, 77, 117
clothing, 45
Companions, xi, 5, 8, 10, 14, 21, 46, 54
concubines, 23, 40–1
consensus, 71, 72–4
Cordoba, 15

Damascus, 5, 90

INDEX

Dananir (Shafi'i's concubine), 40–1
Dawud, al-Zahiri, 31, 91
debate, 74
al-Dhahabi, 35
dictation, 9
Disagreements between 'Ali and 'Abdallah ibn Mas'ud (Shafi'i), 73–4
Disagreements between Hadith (Shafi'i), 52, 53, 58, 61–2, 89, 118
Disagreements between Malik and Shafi'i (Rabi'), 90
Disagreements between the Two Iraqis (Shafi'i), 22, 48, 90
divorce, 28–9, 85–7, 87, 90, 118
Diwan (Collected Poems, Shafi'i), 7, 15, 17, 108
dower, 44, 45, 85–7

East Africa, 95
Egypt, 1, 31–3, 43, 44, 47, 49, 53, 94, 95, 111
El Shamsy, Ahmed, 37–8, 49–50, 53, 68, 73, 80, 81, 93, 115, 118
ethnic hierarchies, 3, 42–3, 67–8
exegesis (*tafsir*), 6, 47, 104

fasting, 71, 84
Fatima, daughter of Muhammad, 4, 109
Fatima, daughter of Shafi'i, 23
Fatima, mother of Shafi'i, 4
Fatimids, 103, 104
Fawz (Shafi'i's slave), 39, 41
finance, 44–6
Fityan ibn Abi Samh, 37–8
food prices, 45
Fustat, 34, 35, 39

Gaza, 2
gender hierarchies, 42–3, 62
al-Ghawri, 104
al-Ghazali, 77, 95
God: communication with humanity (*bayan*), 52, 53, 58–61; humanity's relationship with, 76–7; obedience to, xi, 53, 69; Shafi'i, friend of, 108–9; as sole lawgiver, 76–7; sovereignty, 76–7
Graham, William, 10, 54
grammar, 24, 52, 67
Gum'a, 'Ali, 95

Haddad, G.F., 108
hadith, xi–xii, 53, 57, 58, 60, 108, 113–15; ablution, 66; as authoritative source, 60–1; and jurisprudence, 10–13, 28–9; and *Kitab al-Umm*, 83–4; language and interpretation, 64–6; and Malik ibn Anas, 10–13; reliability of 61–2; and *Risala* (Shafi'i), 52, 55–6, 61–2; *Summation of Knowledge* (Shafi'i), 61; two parts, 9–10; writing, 11
Hafs al-Fard, 75
Hallaq, Wael, 49, 118
Hamida (Shafi'i's wife), 23
Hammad ibn Abi Sulayman, 21
Hanafism, 36, 49, 89, 94, 99
Hanbalis, 94
Harmala ibn Yahya, 18, 34, 93
Harman, Claire, 15
Harun al-Rashid, 5, 15, 19, 44, 119
Hasan ibn 'Ali, 19, 109
al-Hasan al-Basri, 75
al-Hasan ibn Muhammad al-Za'farani, 30, 31
Hashim, 2–3
Heffening, W., xiv
hikma (wisdom), 57–8
Hoffmann-Ladd, Valerie, 102
Hudhayl tribe, 6–7, 14
Hujja (Shafi'i), 30, 34, 48, 89
Humaydi, 'Abdallah ibn al-Zubayr 34–5, 36
Husayn ibn 'Ali, 102

Ibn 'Abd al- A'la, Yunus 34, 83
Ibn 'Abd al-Hakam, 12, 33, 34, 38, 39, 44, 93, 104, 111
Ibn 'Abd al-Hakam family plot, 38, 39, 103
Ibn Abi Hatim al Razi, 1–2, 42, 117
Ibn Abi Layla, 90
Ibn al-Fard, 104
Ibn al-Jawzi, 108
Ibn al-Mundhir, Abu Bakr, 80
Ibn al-Munkadir, 'Isa, 38
Ibn al-Nadim, 17–18, 30
Ibn al-Qasim, 32, 85–6
Ibn Battuta, 106
Ibn Hanbal, 24, 27–9, 30, 36, 46, 75–6, 79, 83, 92, 106, 107, 110

Ibn Hazm, 31
Ibn Jubayr, 106
Ibn Khallikan, 1, 2–3, 7, 43, 49, 104, 106, 107, 111, 117
Ibn Khanbal, 118, 119
Ibn Qadi Shubha, 29, 37, 56, 75, 93
Ibn Qustantin, Isma'il ibn 'Abdullah 4–5
Ibn Rahawayh, 29, 47
Ibn Surayj, Abu'l 'Abbas, 49, 93, 94
Ibn Tulun, Ahmad 36, 94
Ibn 'Ulayya, Ibrahim, 53, 73
Ibn Wahb, 32
Ibrahim al-Nakha'i, 21
ijtihad, 49, 52, 70–2, 73, 76
Indonesia, 95
Inquisition, 77, 93
Invalidation of Juristic Preference (Shafi'i), 48, 90–1
Iraq, 13–15, 19, 21–5, 30–1, 32, 33, 42, 43, 47, 48, 94, 111
'Isa ibn Aban, 49
isnad paradigm, 10
isnads (chains of transmission), 55, 61, 114
Istanbul, 15
istislah, 91

Ja'far al-Sadiq, 109
Jahiz, 68
Jannat al-Baqi, 107
Jaques, Kevin, 35, 110–11
judgeships, 21, 32
jurisprudence, 14, 55, 77, 108; and hadith, 10–13, 28–9; *Kitab al-Umm* (Shafi'i), 84–8
juristic preference, 90–1
al-Juwayni, 95

al-Kabir, 'Ali Bey, 106
Kamali, Mohammad Hashim, 91
al-Karabisi, al-Husayn, 30–1
Keller, Nuh Ha Mim, 95
khabar al-khassa/khabar al-wahid, 73
al-Khatib al-Baghdadi, 30, 31, 107
Khayr al-Din al-Ramli, 99
al-Khushshani, 104
al-Kindi, 32
Kitab al-Umm (Shafi'i), 14, 24, 34, 35, 39, 48, 56, 74, 79; textual history of, 81–2; dower, 85–7; and hadith 83–4; hermeneutical strategies, 82–4; jurisprudence, comparative view, 84–8; legal disagreements, 88–9; literalism, 91–2; paternity, 92; and the Qur'an, 83–4; textual history, 80–1; "touch", use of word, 91–2
Kufa, 21

language, 6, 7, 13, 14, 39; ambiguity, 67; Arabic, 66–8; hadith, 64–6; Qur'an, 64–6, 67–8
law, 113; four-source method of, 51 importance of, xiii; inheritance, 39; and predestination, 76–7; sunna as source of, 59–62; and theology, 74–7
legal hierarchies, 41–2
Lesser Qarafa cemetery, Cairo, 103
livingislam.org, 108
Lowry, Joseph, 51, 58, 59, 61, 67–8, 76, 117, 118

Makdisi, George, 76
Malaysia, 95
al-Malik al-Kamil, 104
Malik ibn Anas, 8, 9, 10–13, 18, 20, 22, 24, 27, 29, 30, 32, 33, 37, 42, 47, 55, 56, 73, 85–6, 88–9, 92, 107, 118, 119
Malikis, 12, 32, 33, 34, 35, 36, 37–8, 85–6, 89–90, 92, 93, 94
Mamluk period, 94
al-Ma'mun, 75
al-Mansur, 5, 15, 21
al-Marisi, Bishr, 44
marriage, 42, 43, 82, 85–7
al-Marwazi, Muhammad al-Hasan ibn Muhammad, 47
al-Marwazi, Muhammad ibn Nasr, 80
Mas'udi, 110
McPherson, Joseph, 109
Mecca, 1, 4, 12, 13, 23, 27, 32, 34–5, 41, 45, 47, 48, 49, 111
medicine, 13, 14
Medina, 1, 5, 8, 12, 111; accepted practice ('*amal*), 11, 22, 33, 55, 73–4
Melchert, Christopher, 35, 77, 80–1, 118
Mughal rule, 94

Muhammad ibn 'Abdallah, 18, 34, 38, 93
Muhammad (Shafi'i's grandson), 7
Muhammad (Shafi'i's son), 23
Muhammad ibn Dawud, 49, 94
Muhammad the Prophet, xii, xvi, 8, 16, 17, 18, 21, 31, 37, 46, 48, 56, 57–8, 60, 76, 83; *see also* sunna
Musa, Aisha, 53, 113, 118
Muslim ibn Hajjaj, 11, 12, 56, 114
Muslim ibn Khalid al-Zanji, 5–6, 33
al-Mutallib, 2–3
Mutarrif ibn Mazin, 14
al-Mutawakkil, 76
Mu'tazilism, 16, 75
al-Muzani, Isma'il ibn Yahya, 35, 36, 37, 39, 43, 49, 81–2, 83, 93–4
Muwatta' [Malik], 8, 9, 10, 12, 22, 56, 118
Muwatta' [Shaybani], 22, 89, 118

Nafisa, Sayyida, 44, 103, 108–9
Najran, 19
al-Nasa'i, xii, 111
Nawas, John, 94
al-Nawawi, 95
Netton, Ian Richard, 106

Oman, 95
opinion, xi–xii, 6, 30, 51, 69, 70, 88, 99
Ottoman empire, 94, 99

Palestine, 1
paternity, 92
pharmacology, 14
physiognomy (*firasa*), 13–14
poetry, 6–7, 14, 17, 39, 108 (See also *Diwan*)
polytheism, 107
prayer, 59–60, 70; female leadership, 110
predestination, 76–7

al-Qadi, Wadad, 13
Qaytbay, 106
qira'a, 9
qiyas, 69–72 (See also analogy)
Qur'an, 52, 53, 54, 59, 69; the Book and the Wisdom, 57–8; createdness, 75–6, 93; dower, 85, 86–7; explanation of all things, 64–5; fasting, 84; illicit sex, 62–4; inheritance law, 39; and the *Kitab al-Umm*, 83–4; language and interpretation, 64–6, 67–8; levels of meaning, 91–2; obedience to Muhammad, 57–8; rules for marriage, 87; as source of law, 72; and sunna, 60–1, 62–4, 113; "touch", use of word, 91–2
Quraysh tribe, 2, 19, 111

Rabi' ibn Sulayman al-Jizi, 35
Rabi' ibn Sulayman al-Muradi, 35–6, 37, 39, 43, 44, 45, 56, 80, 81, 92, 94, 119
Rafidism, 17
Raghib, Yusuf, 109
rape, 87–8
al-Razi, Fakhr al-Din, 14, 49
Refutation of Muhammad ibn al-Hasan [Shaybani] (Shafi'i'), 22, 30, 34, 88, 90
religious learning, 14
revelation, 51, 54, 76–7, 108, 113, 114, 115; gaps in, 70, 91; sunna as, 56–8
Risala (Shafi'i), 33, 117–8; analogy, 51, 52; authorship and authenticity, 48–51; *bayan*, 51, 58–61, 69, 72; chronology, 53; consensus, 49, 52, 72–3; divine communication to humanity, 52; dower, 87; four-source method of Islamic law, 51; and hadith, 52, 55–6, 61–2; *ijtihad*, 52; illicit sex, 62–4; juristic preference, 91; language and interpretation, 52, 64–6; non-contradiction, 52; as outdated, 113; prophetic example, 52, 54–5; *qiyas* and *ijtihad*, 70–2; Qur'an, 51, 52; revelation, 52, 56–8; theological polemic, 76; two versions of, 49

Sa'd ibn Abi Waqqas, 7
Sahnun al-Tanukhi, 85–6
Sahnun ibn Sa'id al-Tanukhi, 32
Sa'ib ibn 'Ubayd, 3
Salafi movement, 95
Saladin (Salah al-Din), 103–4
Salih (slave), 42
Salim (slave), 42
sama' (hearing), 9

al-Sari ibn al-Hakam, 32, 37, 110
Schacht, Joseph, 20, 118
Schoeler, Gregor, 9
science, 108
sex, illicit, 62–4, 88
Shafi'i: annual birthday celebrations, 102; birth of, 1–2; death of, 38–9; early education, 4–6; father's ancestry, 2–3; friend of God, 108–9; funeral, 109–10; intercessor, 102, 115; legal scholarship, 21–5; marriage, 23; martial training, 6–7; mother's ancestry, 4; professional relationships with women, 43–4; as renewer of the faith, 115; veneration of, 110–11; will, 39–44, 44; *see also* individual works
al-Shafi'i, Abu 'Abd al-Rahman, 31
Shafi' ibn al-Sa'ib, 41
Shafi'i school, 34–7, 93–6
Shafi'i, tomb of: building, 103–6; decoration, 106; letters, 101–2; pilgrimages to, 99–101; spiritual benefits, 99, 104
Shahrazuri, 56
Shaybani, Muhammad, 12, 20, 22–3, 24–5, 30, 32, 34, 45, 85, 88, 89, 90, 118, 119
Shi'a, 16
Shu'ubiyya movement, 16
Siyar al-Awza'i (Abu Yusuf), 90
slaves, 23, 40–1, 42, 63, 82, 88
social etiquette, 83
South Asia, 114
Spectorsky, Susan A., 27, 118
Stewart, Devin, 49
al-Subki, Taj al-Din, 37
Successors, 8
Sufism, 108
Sufyan ibn 'Uyayna, 6, 28, 29, 33, 34, 44
Summation of Knowledge (Shafi'i), 48, 51, 52–3, 55, 58, 59, 113, 118; Arabic language, 67; consensus, 73; illicit sex, 63–5; *qiyas* and *ijtihad*, 70–2; reliability of hadith, 61; theology, 74–7
sunna, xi–xii, 11, 29, 31, 34, 59, 69, 71, 108; ablution, 66; contradictions in, 65–6; fasting, 84; illicit sex, 63–5; and Malik ibn Anas, 11; and Qur'an, 60–1, 62–4, 113; as revelation, 56–8; as source of law, 59–62, 72; varying levels of command, 65–6
Syria, 90, 94, 95

al-Tabari, 19, 119
al-Tahawi, 36, 43
tawatur, 72, 73
al-Thaqafi, 'Abd al-Wahhab ibn 'Abd al-Majid, 24
theology, 24, 52, 91, 74–7 (see also Mu'tazilism)
Tirmidhi, 29
tombs, visiting, ix, xiii, 99–101, 106–7

'Umar ibn al-Khattab, 17, 54
'Umar ibn 'Abd al-Aziz, 115
Umayyads, 5, 18, 90
Umm, the (Shafi'i) *see Kitab al-Umm* (Shafi'i)
'Uthman ibn 'Affan, 17, 23
'Uways, Sayyid, 101, 102

Vaujany, H. de, 106
Virtues (Manaqib), xiv
Vishanoff, David, 67

Wasil ibn 'Ata', 75
Williams, Caroline, 103
women: free, 42, 63, 88; and prayer, 110; professional, 43–4; *see also* concubines; dower; marriage
worship, 83

Yahya ibn 'Abdallah, 19, 23
Yemen, 1, 2, 13–15, 44, 95, 111; 'Alid partisanship, 19–20
Yunani, 6–7

al-Zahir Barquq, 104
Zahiris, 31
Zayd ibn 'Ali, 18, 34
Zaynab (Shafi'i's daughter), 23, 43
Zaynab, Sayyida, 102
Zaytuna Institute, 109
Zuhriya (Shafi'i's wife), 23